GET-REAL VEGAN DESSERTS

THE TRAVELING GOURMAND SERIES

1. *The Gluten-Free Way: My Way*, by William Maltese & Adrienne Z. Milligan
2. *Back of the Boat Gourmet Cooking: Afloat—Pool-Side—Backyard*, by Bonnie Clark & William Maltese
3. *William Maltese's Wine Taster's Diary: Spokane/Pullman Washington Wine Region*, by William Maltese
4. *In Search of the Perfect Pinot G! Australia's Mornington Peninsula: William Maltese's Wine Taster's Guide #2*, by A. B. Gayle & William Maltese
5. *Whole Wheat for Food Storage: Recipes for Unground Wheat*, by Michael R. Collings & Judith Collings
6. *Even Gourmands Have to Diet: It's Just Food, People!*, by Bonnie Clark and William Maltese
7. *Dinner with Cecile and William: A Cookbook*, by Cecile Charles and William Maltese
8. *The Pot Thickens: Recipes from the Kitchens of Writers and Readers*, edited by Victor J. Banis
9. *Get-Real Vegan Desserts: Vegan Recipes for the Rest of Us*, by Christina-Marie "Sexy Vegan Mama" Wright and William Maltese

GET-REAL VEGAN DESSERTS

VEGAN RECIPES FOR THE REST OF US

CHRISTINA-MARIE WRIGHT & WILLIAM MALTESE

THE BORGO PRESS
MMXIII

THE TRAVELING GOURMAND
NUMBER NINE

GET-REAL VEGAN DESSERTS

Copyright © 2013 by Christina-Marie Wright and
William Maltese
Cover Art by Christina-Marie Wright

FIRST EDITION

Published by Wildside Press LLC

www.wildsidebooks.com

DEDICATION

CHRISTINA-MARIE—

For my mother, Melody, at whose knee I learned to bake (yes, I know how clichéed that sounds), who always answers the phone when a cake collapses or a frosting flops, and without whom this book could not have been written. Thanks, Mom, for holding my hand throughout my vegan journey. I'm privileged to walk with you.

WILLIAM MALTESE—

To my co-author, Christina-Marie "Sexy Vegan Mama" Wright, without whose expertise there's no way this book could/would have seen the light of day.

CONTENTS

AUTHORS' NOTE. 9
CHAPTER ONE: BEFORE WE VEGAN. 11
CHAPTER TWO: HISTORY OF VEGANISM . . 15
CHAPTER THREE: WHO'S EATING VEGAN,
    AND WHY 18
CHAPTER FOUR: YES, VIRGINIA, THERE
    REALLY IS A VEGAN CREAM CHEESE . . 26
CHAPTER FIVE: A NOTE ABOUT SOY
    FOODS AND GMO'S 33
CHAPTER SIX: THE INGREDIENTS 34
CHAPTER SEVEN: WHAT? SUGAR ISN'T
    VEGAN?! 40
CHAPTER EIGHT: WHAT ABOUT HONEY?. . 43
COOKIES AND BISCOTTI 44
CHEESECAKES AND TORTES 60
CAKES, CUPCAKES, BROWNIES AND
    FROSTINGS 74

PIES, PASTIES, AND CRISPS 88
BAKING WITH PHYLLO 114
DOUGHNUTS AND OTHER DEEP-FRIED
  SINS. 123
FROZEN FANCIES 136
CANDIES AND MUNCHIES 145
CINNAMON ROLLS AND DESSERT BREADS 164
VEGAN BLOGS THE COOL KIDS READ . . 173
GET SCHOOLED: ONLINE VEGAN
  RESOURCES 178
ACKNOWLEDGEMENTS AND SHOUT-
  OUTS 181
ABOUT THE AUTHORS: YOU CAN'T
  MAKE THIS STUFF UP 184

AUTHORS' NOTE

This book is not intended to provide medical advice. Proper diagnosis of food allergies, sensitivities, cholesterol levels or any other medical conditions needs to be sought out from the appropriate medical professionals. When choosing a vegan diet, consult with a nutritional expert to evaluate your personal dietary needs. All contents of this book are the personal experiences and opinions of the authors.

****

All organizations, businesses and product names mentioned in this book are the property of those individual organizations and businesses. In this day and age of the internet when so many organizations, businesses, and products are so often made mention of without their attending trademark designates ™ ®, it's difficult to know when or if to provide these indicators. Even specific searches of U.S. Trademark Department files can often be confusing. So, more often than not, the authors have erred on the side of inclusion, rather than exclusion. If mistakes have been made, we shall make every attempt to make sure they're corrected in any subsequent editions of this book.

CHAPTER ONE: BEFORE WE VEGAN

What Veganism Is, and What This Book Is Not

vegan:

a person who does not consume, use or eat any animal products; a supporter of veganism

veganism:

the practice of eating neither meat nor other animal products, such as fish, milk and milk products, eggs, and honey; a way of life which strictly avoids use of any kind of animal products and services that are based on exploitation of animals (Source: http://en.wiktionary.org)

Christina-Marie's goal in collaborating with William on this cookbook is to create a simple, realistic tool for busy parents, those new to a vegan diet, people with egg or dairy allergies, folks watching their cholesterol, and traditional foodies who would consider a vegan diet if only it weren't so intimidating.

The first vegan cookbooks Christina-Marie

purchased were filled with bizarre-sounding ingredients like xanthan gum, agar agar, agave nectar, and other things she couldn't find at her local grocery. Of course, that was almost fifteen years ago, and large retail supermarkets have come a long way in stocking natural foods and vegan options since then. Even in her very rural area, she can usually request special orders through her grocer and small natural foods store. See Chapter 4 for tips on getting your local store to stock vegan products.

Choosing a vegan diet is a personal decision for every individual, and each has his or her own reasons. Some are allergic to eggs, dairy, or animal proteins. A doctor may recommend a vegan diet for patients with high cholesterol, because cholesterol is only found in animal-sourced foods. Many call themselves "ethical vegans," citing a personal desire to reduce animal suffering and exploitation. Some choose a vegan diet for environmental reasons, declaring that the raising of livestock contributes to air and water pollution. Still others believe a global shift toward a vegan diet can solve the world hunger problem, claiming plant-based agriculture makes better use of natural resources and produces more food per square foot than the raising of livestock.

Veganism, for many, is about more than food choices. "Abolitionist vegans" strive to end the exploitation and killing of all animals by the food, clothing, entertainment and other industries.

While several vegans share their personal reasons

for enjoying a vegan diet in Chapter 3, this cookbook is not intended to decry or condemn anyone's food or lifestyle choices.

In fact, this book is NOT...

...intended to be misconstrued as medical advice.

...a handbook or manifesto on abolitionist veganism. The views expressed by interviewees or recommended resources are those of the individual, not of the authors.

...a diet or weight-loss book. With these rich desserts? Are you kidding?

...full of weird or hard-to-find ingredients. Most can be found at any large supermarket. Get tips on finding vegan ingredients in Chapter 4.

...for expert chefs only. Indeed, Christina-Marie has no formal baking experience or training, outside hanging around her mom's bakery as a young teen. Even then, she was pretty much just waiting for cute guys to come in and buy doughnuts. Christina-Marie, that is. Not her mother.

...a very large advertisement for any particular company or product. If we name a product, it is only to identify a brand that may be widely available or easy to obtain for those not living in large metropolitan areas. It's not because they're lining our pockets to pimp their product.

...an endorsement of any company's practices, ethics or manufacturing processes. If abolitionist veganism is a lifestyle you embrace, please research each manufacturer to determine if their policies align with your personal beliefs. If you have significant food sensitivities, please contact individual companies to ascertain whether cross-contamination is possible during the manufacturing process. Just because a product is egg-free, for example, doesn't mean the equipment it is manufactured on isn't also used to process ingredients containing eggs.

...a stale, old-school-recipe book. We aim to inform and entertain. We believe food should be a celebration. Let's get the party started!

CHAPTER TWO: HISTORY OF VEGANISM

The Garden of Vegan—and Beyond

According to Wikipedia—and we all know that anything found on Wikipedia is almost true—"the avoidance of meat can be traced to India, and to the Pythagoreans and Orphics in ancient Greece." Indeed, the common term for a diet free of fish and meat was "The Pythagorean Diet" until the word "vegetarian" was coined in the nineteenth century. Pythagoras and his followers chose their diet for religious and metaphysical reasons. Namely, they believed souls could transmigrate from one body to another. (Source: http://en.wikipedia.org/wiki/Pythagoreans)

Seriously, who wants to share soul space with a cow?

From *Life of Pythagoras,* by Diogenes Laertius:

A state of purity is brought about by purifications, washings and lustrations, by a man's purifying himself from all deaths and rebirths, or any kind of pollution, by abstaining from all animals that have died, from mullets, from gurnards, from eggs, from such animals that lay eggs, from beans, and from other things that are prohibited by those who have charge of the mysteries in the Temples.

Christina-Marie, personally, would like to second Pythagoras's abstention from mullets. They're a fashion travesty, and have no place in a sexy vegan's world.

The work excerpted above further reveals Pythagoras was tolerant of, and even indulged in, cheese and honey, so he was vegetarian, not vegan, but for a guy who set up his philosophy practice around 530 B.C./B.C.E., he was a pretty progressive thinker.

The Bible—which some consider just as reliable as Wikipedia—reveals a truly vegan diet was created in the Garden of Eden, right around the time Adam and Eve likely developed a hankerin' for something to satisfy the rumbling in their newly-formed tummies. God had had a very busy sixth day, creating man and woman, but He still had to feed them. So, He whipped up everything the couple would need to eat, right there in the Garden. When finished, He said to them, "...Behold, I have given you every herb bearing seed, which is upon the face of all the earth, and every tree, in which is the fruit of a tree yielding seed; to you it shall be for meat." (Genesis 1:29, King James Version)

As Christina-Marie's friend Catherine Burt —a.k.a. In-A-Gadda-Da-Vegan—says, "Paradise was vegan."

Sadly, it didn't last. Adam and Eve made a major faux pas, earning them a one-way ticket out of Eden. As humanity spread over the earth, so did evil. In fact, just a few short biblical chapters later, God made an executive decision to flood the earth, destroying all life except what He instructed an obedient man named Noah to cram into an ark. With everything underwater, there was neither seed nor fruit available, so God changed His mind about eating the animals: "Every moving thing that liveth shall be meat for you; even as the green herb have I given you all things." (Genesis 9:3, King James Version)

Fast-forward a few millennia to 1847 England, where an enlightened chap named Joseph Brotherton coined the term "vegetarian" to describe folks who didn't eat flesh. Until 1944, those who also avoided eggs, dairy, and other animal products were simply known as "strict vegetarians." For all their dedication, those strict vegetarians should be honored with their own descriptive title, don't you think? Donald Watson and his wife, Dorothy, certainly thought so, and in 1944 developed the term "vegan," combining the first three and last two letters of the word "vegetarian." As Watson described it, the term was "the beginning and end of vegetarian." (Source: http://en.wikipedia.org/wiki/Veganism)

Today, veganism is practiced by conscientious people across the globe and, since 1994, World Vegan Day is celebrated on November 1 of each year. Other international vegan observances and events include Worldwide Vegan Bake Sale week (http://www.VeganBakeSale.org) and Vegan Month of Food, affectionately known as VeganMoFo (http://VeganMoFo.wordpress.com).

CHAPTER THREE: WHO'S EATING VEGAN, AND WHY

The reasons for choosing a vegan diet and lifestyle are as varied as the individuals opting for them. Some cite health, weight loss, or allergy reasons; while others are convicted by an ethical or moral calling.

Christina-Marie, your Sexy Vegan Mama, made the decision to stop eating animals at age fourteen—after surviving sexual trauma. She'd drawn a parallel between food and pleasure, and found she could no longer justify the killing of animals to satisfy her pleasure. As a sexual abuse victim, she'd been harmed by another individual in order to satisfy a particular pleasure or lust, and she just couldn't bring herself to harm another creature in order to satisfy her "lust" for food, and the pleasure she received from it.

After several years of opting for a meat-free diet, she realized animal suffering didn't always result in death. Independently studying the practices at large commercial egg and dairy farms finally made veganism the only option for her, but it took time.

Learning about the de-beaking of chickens forced into battery cages, where their claws grow around the wires, was enough to determine her conscience about eggs. (Learn more at http://www.eggindustry.com.)

When her son became old enough to drink milk, she became concerned about reports she'd read about the Bovine Growth Hormone (BGH) being given to dairy cows, causing many to develop *mastitis*, an inflammation of the milk ducts. As many nursing mothers know, mastitis is extremely painful, resulting in rock-hard breasts that are hot to the touch.

To be clear, Christina-Marie doesn't mean "hot, rock-hard breasts" in a sexy way. It's not pleasant.

Anyway, mastitis is treated with antibiotics, and Christina-Marie became concerned about the dosage of antibiotics her son was consuming with each glass of milk. Would he develop a tolerance? What would happen if he became ill and required antibiotics? Would he have to take larger and larger doses to reap the benefits?

Even organic, BGH-free milk didn't ease her conscience when she learned of the plight of most dairy cows. These poor mamas are repeatedly artificially inseminated to force them to produce milk to feed their newborn calves—but their babies are quickly removed, sometimes immediately after birth. The females are raised to endure the lives their mothers live, while the males are whisked away to be raised as beef or—even worse—as veal.

While a healthy cow can expect to live over twenty years, the lifespan of a dairy cow is about four years. After that, she's no longer profitable to the farmer due to her body no longer producing "adequate" milk levels after the repeated cycle of forced insemination and lactation. When she can't keep up the expected milk production, the dairy cow is sent to slaughter, made into hamburger or pet food, because her body is too worn to be of any further value. (Learn more at http://www.milksucks.com.)

The one food Christina-Marie thought she could never give up was cheese. How could she never, ever enjoy another pizza? Or the simplicity and comfort of a grilled cheese sandwich with tomato soup? Then, she found out how cheese is actually made, and her vegetarian heaven came crashing down. Boy, did she ever feel like Chicken Little when she learned the milk in most cheeses is coagulated and solidified by the addition of *rennet*. For those not familiar with the ingredient, prepare to chuck your cheese.

Rennet is an enzyme taken from the lining of stomachs of nursing baby animals. The purpose of rennet is to help the suckling babies digest their mothers' milk. Therefore, the type of rennet used in a particular cheese is determined by the type of milk used to make the cheese: cow milk cheeses use rennet from the stomachs of calves, goat milk cheeses add rennet from baby goats, sheep milk cheeses contain rennet from lambs, and so on.

While vegetable-sourced rennet is available, it isn't widely used in the commercial cheese industry. Christina-Marie's sister-in-law, for example, uses vegetable rennet to make cheese from her much-loved, spoiled-rotten milk cow. The cow is spoiled, not the milk.

Needless to say, Christina-Marie's cheese addiction was cured, instantly. Baby stomach extract? No, thank you. In this way, she became vegan over time, and her heart always took the lead.

She's been blessed to know and meet many vegans through the wonder of the internet, and each has his or her own reason for veganism. Here are some stories from friends:

Kris Miller, of DustpanProductions.com, has been vegan since March 2010. She came to veganism as a method of detoxification from Candidiasis, eczema, and Chronic Fatigue Syndrome. Due to her food sensitivities, Kris also eats gluten-free, stays away from refined foods, and eats predominately organics. [See William's book (with Adrienne Z. Hoffman)—*THE GLUTEN-FREE WAY: MY WAY.*]

While Kris cites expense and constant trips to the grocery for fresh produce among her biggest challenges in maintaining her diet, she credits her veganism and other food choices for making her body healthier.

Kristi Arnold, of VeggieConverter.com, has been vegetarian since 1991, and "trying to be vegan" since 2009. Initially, Kristi stopped eating meat because she simply didn't like it. Even as a baby, she rejected baby food with meat in it. When she became a nursing mother, Kristi "began to understand how odd it is that we should eat and drink animal milk."

Kristi's family remains omnivorous, and meal

preparation is a challenge. Sometimes, it's a matter of doing things buffet-style—meat toppings for some, not for others. Regarding her dietary choices, she says, "It's really pretty simple. If you don't like meat or don't want to use animal products, just don't. It's not hard, once you put your mind to it. It just takes planning... you feel a lot better about yourself, and can be a lot healthier!"

Kyle Domer, who blogs at VeganVagrant.com, has been vegan since 2002. To explain what led him to a vegan diet, Kyle says, "I was overweight, tired, sluggish, lazy and without clear focus. I tried vegetarianism and found that it was not helpful in the least the way I did it, because I was just overloading on carbs and dairy. I was sick and tired of being sick and tired. I switched to veganism and lost 45 pound in four months. My mind felt clearer, I had bursting energy and required less sleep, but somehow always felt more rested and energized. I started for selfish reasons, but since then have come to also embrace and appreciate the positive impact on animals and the environment."

After nearly a decade of veganism, Kyle finds absolutely no challenges to maintaining and constantly expanding his diet. "There are so many amazing products and recipes available to vegans it's impossible to say that it's 'hard' to be vegan, especially in Southern California," he says. That's one of the main objectives of his blog—to show that everywhere one goes, vegan options are not only easy and accessible, but also downright delicious.

What does Kyle want the world to know about veganism? "It's easy, healthy if done correctly, fun, creative and all around the single best decision a person can make for the benefit of themselves, animals and the environment."

Robbie Gleeson, on Twitter at http://twitter.com/itsjustrobbieok, has been raw vegan since Boxing Day 2010. That is, Robbie only eats vegan foods, and he doesn't eat them heated above 104°F (40° C). According to Wikipedia's article on Raw Foodism (http://en.wikipedia.org/wiki/Raw_foodism):

Raw vegans such as Dr. Douglas Graham believe that foods cooked above this temperature have lost much of their nutritional value and are less healthy or even harmful to the body. Raw or living foods have natural enzymes, which are critical in building proteins and rebuilding the body. Heating these foods kills the natural enzymes, and can leave toxins behind. Typical foods include fruit, vegetables, nuts, seeds and sprouted grains and legumes.

Robbie read *The China Study* by T. Colin Campbell, Ph.D. and Thomas M. Campbell II, a book on how nutrition and diet are linked to heart disease, diabetes, and cancer. He continued to research on his own, and found reports of people feeling amazing and healthier after becoming vegan. As an athlete, Robbie hoped to feel better and achieve better performance in his sports. After going raw, he admits the smell of cooked foods still causes his mouth to water, but he finds his raw vegan diet makes him feel great, and powers his body "pretty damn well," and tastes good, too!

Tracye Mayolo has been vegan since Thanksgiving 2010. After reading a great article in a natural health magazine citing three majors reasons for becoming vegan—humane treatment of animals, environmental benefits and personal health—Tracye was relieved to learn veganism didn't have to be a "cold turkey" decision, but could be made through good choices, one meal at a time. A comment by her ten-year-old daughter, Maggie, at Thanksgiving dinner, "Why do the cute animals have to taste so good?" contributed to her decision to go vegan.

Tracye likes experimenting, trying new things, and making choices that are better for her health and the environment. She doesn't like the thought of how inhumanely animals are treated as meat is mass-produced. While her vegan diet sometimes causes her to feel "on her own" and segregated during social mealtimes, she sticks to her beliefs, and respects those of others. As Tracye says, "It's just like religion. Be sensitive to, and respect, diversity. We all have our beliefs. Give people the room to believe in and eat what they want—even if it's not traditional."

Catherine Burt, a.k.a. In-A-Gadda-Da-Vegan, blogs at http://blogs.standard.net/in-a-gadda-da-vegan. Like many others, Catherine's first step toward veganism was adopting an ovo-lacto vegetarian diet. "...After a few years of waffling," she says, "I knew it wasn't the best I could do, either for myself, the environment, or the animals."

With a rich social life that includes many vegan friends and a vegan mate, Catherine says family members tend to eat a bit healthier when they're around her, and they see she's healthier, herself, due to sticking to her plant-based diet.

"Veganism is a big party," says Catherine, "and you're ALL invited!"

CHAPTER FOUR: YES, VIRGINIA, THERE REALLY IS A VEGAN CREAM CHEESE

Vegan Ingredients, and How to Get Them

When Christina-Marie adopted a vegan diet more than fifteen years ago, vegan alternatives to her favorite foods were scarce. Or, if they did exist, they tasted... well, "vegan." Dairy-free cheeses had the flavor quotient and consistency of cardboard, didn't melt, and were proportionately expensive. Vegan cream cheese substitutes had a plastic-like quality, and soy yogurt had a decidedly "tofu" taste. The same could be said about her early experiences with soy-based "ice creams."

We're happy to report that's all changed, and vegan equivalents for traditionally animal-derived standards are getting better every day.

Today, companies are producing game-changing products that look, taste and behave like "the real thing." Pizza is no longer a fond memory with dairy-free "cheese" shreds like Daiya Deliciously Dairy-

Free®, grilled cheese sandwiches make a comeback with products like Galaxy Nutritional Foods Vegan Slices®, and Vegan Gourmet® makes block cheeses that can be sliced, grated or melted for use in a wide variety of dishes.

In creating desserts, we use many vegan alternatives to butter, cream cheese, marshmallows, sour cream, milk, sugar and more. (More on vegan sugars in Chapter 7.) These products aren't difficult to find, if you're in a major metropolitan area. If you're lucky enough to live within hollerin' distance of a Whole Foods Market or similar natural foods-friendly chain grocer, vegan alternatives are already waiting for you to scoop them into your organic cotton shopping bag.

So, what about the folks like Christina-Marie, who live in rural America, opting for open spaces and beauty over convenience and mass-transit?

Don't lose hope. Getting your nimble vegan hands on these fine products may require a bit of ingenuity and planning, but it's not impossible. In fact, it's even easier if you have a network of vegan friends who can split large-quantity orders with you, so don't be shy about connecting with other vegans in your area.

For the purposes of this book, we'll be discussing three different venues through which to obtain your vegan treasures:

Small, independent natural foods stores or grocers.

Larger chain grocers who may not regularly cater to vegan clientele.

Shopping online through vegan websites.

Your Local Indie Natural Foods Store or Grocer: Support Your Community

Just because your local indie foods stores are small doesn't mean they don't have connections or ordering power. Perhaps, like Christina-Marie's favorite independent natural foods store, Bear Foods of Chelan, Washington, they just don't have enough demand to warrant stocking certain items on their shelves. Remember that every product in inventory is an expense for your shop owner until it sells.

We like to patronize local independent businesses whenever possible. According to Indiebound.org, when you spend $100.00 at a local business, $68.00 stays in your local community, compared to $43.00 of every $100.00 spent at a national chain store. Shopping local also means more taxes get reinvested in your local community, and local jobs are created for community members.

The benefits of patronizing local independent shops don't end there. Indie-bound claims shopping local helps the environment, because less packaging and fossil fuels are involved in transportation. For example, Christina-Marie's local natural foods store stocks and sells local produce and handmade goods, whenever possible.

Best of all, shopping at a small local store means a direct connection to the owners and employees. When Christina-Marie walks through the door of Bear Foods, folks know her by name—and not just because her face appears next to her newspaper column in the local newspaper. They know if her order has come in, which new products in which she's likely to be interested, and which vitamins, liquid pain relievers and fruit snacks are free of the red dye to which her kids are allergic.

So, when she needs a particular ingredient, she asks the inventory manager at Bear Foods to order it for her. Sometimes, if it's a product the manager doesn't feel will sell quickly enough, she'll ask Christina-Marie to buy an entire case or other minimum order so the manager won't end up sitting on inventory that can't be sold.

This is where having a circle of vegan friends comes in handy. Perhaps Christina-Marie can't use a case of vegan marshmallows (actually, she probably could, so great is her love for marshmallows), but she can certainly split a case with four friends.

Your Local Retail Chain Supermarket: Use Their Buying Power

As you can see from the explanation above, bigger isn't always better. However, if your local independent food store can't order what you need for some reason, it's worth a shot to approach your local retail chain store. In many cases, the larger store may be able to access your product at a lower price than an independent shop. Your personal finances and world view will determine if cost is the most important element in acquiring and buying vegan products.

Christina-Marie has successfully sweet-talked her local retail grocer into carrying specific items by filling out comment cards, leaving feedback online at the corporate website, and speaking with department managers. The last technique has proven by far the most effective, perhaps because the manager is forced to see her adorable, pouty face when the grocer even considers saying that the store can't order an item. It also helps if you, like Christina-Marie, have seven children you can crowd into the manager's office. At that point, even the most resistant non-vegan usually breaks down and does whatever it takes to get such a brood out of his or her proximity.

In all seriousness, most managers will be receptive to your request. After all, they want you to shop in their store, and through your request they may see they're missing out on potential sales from vegan consumers. Even if the store is not willing to stock your specific product on a regular basis, they may be willing to place a special order for you—provided you purchase the entire case or minimum packaging quantity. Again, it's nice to have friends who will split the order and expense with you, if at all possible.

Christina-Marie has launched successful comment card and website feedback campaigns, resulting in her local retail chain store carrying certain items, but it required organization, determination and persistence she doesn't always have time for these days (did we mention her seven children?). Still, it's possible.

First, fill out a comment card at the store's customer service counter, explaining that you walked into the store, hoping to find a specific product, but were unable to locate it. Describe the product with as much detail as possible, including a brand name, so the inventory clerk can search for it through the store's suppliers. Express your desire for the store to carry the product. Add that you enjoy shopping there, and would like to be able to complete your shopping, in its entirety, within one store. Be sure to include your contact information so the manager can call or email you with questions – or to let you know your product is now on the shelves of the store.

Ask your friends—whether vegan or not—to fill out comment cards requesting the product, and fill out a new comment card each time you shop. Locate the corporate website for the company, and leave similar feedback through the customer service link. Send emails to your friends, with feedback they can copy and paste, along with a link to the corporate customer service department. When your local chain sees several comment cards requesting a specific item, it's bound to trigger a proactive response. Likewise, if the corporate center sees a spike in requests for a particular product, it may make sense for the company to start stocking the item or brand on a national scale.

What? What's that? That sounds like a lot of work, and will take a long time? You're right. It certainly can, as almost all grassroots movements do. Don't let that dissuade you, though! While you're working your campaign, you can always order products online to tide you over until your ultimate goal of global retail renovation takes place.

Ordering Online: Specialty Vegan Items with a Few Keystrokes and a Click

If you have internet access, the ability to plan ahead, and the patience to wait on shipping, ordering online is an excellent option for purchasing products you can't find near you. The upside is almost anything can be found online. The downside is waiting for your order to arrive, and paying shipping and handling charges. Of course, if you live in rural America, like Christina-Marie does, there's a fuel expense involved in driving to a store, anyway.

A few online sources for vegan products are:

Vegan Essentials at veganessentials.com—Vegan-owned and -operated; does not sell anything tested on animals or containing any animal products, great source for vegan whipped cream, marshmallows and baking mixes

Pangea, The Vegan Store at www.veganstore.com—Sells only goods from countries that have labor laws in place to protect workers against sweatshop industry; prides itself on being a cruelty-free source for shopping, excellent selection of vegan "cheeses" and other dairy-free spreads and products

Amazon at amazon.com—Carries select vegan products, many in large quantities; good for wholecase discounts

This list is by no means exhaustive, and if you're outside the United States, you will, no doubt, have different sites to choose from. These are simply some of our favorites.

CHAPTER FIVE: A NOTE ABOUT SOY FOODS AND GMO'S

Soy products have come under heavy fire in recent years, as soybeans (along with corn) are among some of the most heavily genetically modified foods on the market. When shopping, I look for products that are non-Genetically Modified Organisms (non-GMO) certified or verified. Companies that shun GMOs are usually proud to label their products as non-GMO, so look for the printed bragging rights.

CHAPTER SIX: THE INGREDIENTS

We'll be using some vegan substitutes in this cookbook, and now that you know how to get them, let's get down to particulars, shall we?

Butter Alternatives

Whether in pie crust, cookies or frosting, butter is a common staple in any baker's refrigerator. Margarine is a viable substitute in most cases, but most commercial margarines rely on whey or other milk proteins to make them creamy and smooth.

Earth Balance® Vegan Buttery Sticks are versatile and easy to use, if you can find a convenient and affordable source for them. We've taken to using a commercial stick margarine which is, as Christina-Marie likes to say, "accidentally vegan." That is, its ingredients are vegan, but it's not marketed as a vegan product. You can find Nucoa® at nearly all retail chain grocers, and it easily adapts to our recipes.

Cream Cheese Alternatives

Cream cheese was one of the foods Christina-Marie most missed when she became vegan. A bagel just didn't taste right without a smooth layer of cream cheese swiped across the top, and she suffered what seemed an eternity of naked bagels before finding Tofutti Better Than Cream Cheese®. This little tub of heaven combines tofu, soybean oil, locust bean, non-dairy lactic acid and other ingredients to produce a passable vegan alternative to cream cheese. Tofutti also offers a blend without hydrogenated oils.

Another vegan cream-cheese alternative is Vegan Gourmet Cream Cheese Alternative® by Follow Your Heart®. At about the same price as Tofutti's product, Vegan Gourmet boasts a higher percentage of organic ingredients and zero hydrogenated oils.

Sour Cream Alternatives

Like its cream cheese cousin, vegan sour cream has come a long way in taste, consistency, and texture. Some of our favorites are Tofutti Sour Supreme® and its non-hydrogenated counterpart, Tofutti Better Than Sour Cream®. Again, Vegan Gourmet® also makes an excellent, mostly-organic competitor.

Our personal preference is for convenience, and in Christina-Marie's part of the country, Tofutti® products are easier to come by than Vegan Gourmet®, so she uses the former most often. Both brands are comparable in cost, and the added bonus of organic ingredients in Vegan Gourmet® products is certainly not snub-worthy.

Milk Alternatives

If you're allergic to soy, you're reading the wrong book. We use soy milk and soy-based dairy alternatives at every turn. That being said, if you have a preference for non-soy milk, feel free to experiment with nut milks, like cashew or almond, or grain milks like rice or oat. Also, we've heard of bakers getting good results with hemp milk, but it's not readily available and can be expensive, so we haven't experimented much with that one.

The primary variable in milk substitutes that will enhance or destroy a recipe is "body." That is, how watery is the milk, and how will it affect baking time or measurement? A bit of trial-and-error will answer these questions. Baking times may need to be increased for milks with less body, and measurements may need to be decreased for thinner milks when adding them to frostings or sauces.

In creating these recipes, we've used Silk® Vanilla Soymilk; full-fat, because Christina-Marie is genuinely comfortable with the size of her present "caboose". Silk® is widely available at most retail locations, is non-GMO, and it does come in a lower-calorie "light" variety. Again, a bit of adjustment may be necessary in some recipes, if you opt for the light version.

Yogurt Alternatives

Good soy-based yogurts provide body, a smooth consistency, and that famous yogurt "tang." We use WholeSoy & Co.® vanilla soy yogurt, because it's available in an economical, 24-ounce size at our local grocery stores, and it's non-GMO verified. Other vegan soy yogurts are produced by Nancy's®, and other companies.

Be careful in selecting your soy yogurt to ensure the cultures are not grown in milk, as some companies—who shall, for purposes of this book, remain nameless in their non-vegan shame—use milk-grown cultures, added to a soy base.

Egg Alternatives

There are a ton of "make your own" egg replacer recipes out there. Some call for flax seed, some call for agar agar, and still others call for fruit or combinations of multiple ingredients.

In our experiences, none are as reliable in baking as a powdered egg replacer, which takes over both the binding and leavening duties of eggs in a recipe. The most common and easy-to-find brand is Ener-G® Egg Replacer, available in the natural foods or baking section of many groceries, or available online at http://www.ener-g.com/egg-replacer.html. Ener-G® was used to develop the recipes in this cookbook.

Vegan Chocolate

When chocolate is needed in this book, you'll find the recipes call for vegan chocolate chips. Finding vegan chocolate may seem an impossible task as you cruise your grocery aisles and see shelves and bins stocked full of "semi-sweet milk chocolate chips," but don't despair. Simply check ingredient lists very carefully, and you may find that even some name-brand chocolate companies have chips lacking dairy, even though they're not marketed as such.

Additionally, several vegan-marketed chocolate chips brands are out there, including Tropical Source®, Sunspire® and Enjoy Life®. Notably, Enjoy Life® chips are not only dairy-free, but also soy- and gluten-free.

For some of the recipes, we've used Xocai® "Healthy Chocolate" products. The health benefits of Xocai® are undeniable—it's full of antioxidants, minerals and flavonols— but please note not all Xocai® products are vegan-friendly. As always, read labels. Xocai® is cold-processed, preserving the natural healthy properties of cacao. When using Xocai® in baking, take care not to warm the product above 100 degrees, in order to preserve all those fantastic health benefits.

Baking Mixes

All-purpose baking mixes rock! A single box yields the promise of pancakes, waffles, biscuits, scones, breads and much, much more. Any cook's dream, right? The problem is that some contain dairy or egg ingredients.

Wholesome Chow® makes a vegan all-purpose baking mix, as do Arrowhead Mills® and The Pure Pantry®. Unfortunately, Christina-Marie doesn't see these brands on the shelves of her local grocery, and she can't always make a trip to her favorite natural-foods store when the baking bug bites.

Bisquick® Heart Smart is free of dairy and egg products, leaving only the low-listed "sugar" to wonder about. We don't know the source of the sugar used in the Bisquick® brand, or if it is treated with bone char. We have, however, found about a million or so recipe websites proclaiming "it's vegan!" So, we've chosen to adopt that popular opinion, and used the Bisquick® HeartSmart mix in developing the pertinent recipes in this book.

CHAPTER SEVEN: WHAT? SUGAR ISN'T VEGAN?!

Walk down the baking aisle of your grocery store and pick up a bag or box of sugar. Then, read the ingredients. You'll most likely see a short list, namely, "100% pure cane sugar," or something to that effect. No beef extract, milk protein, egg or other animal products means it's vegan, right?

In actuality, no.

Most of the white stuff that passes for sugar isn't vegan. Most granulated white cane sugar in the United States is refined with bone char, a granular material made—appropriately enough—by charring animal bones.

Why? To make it that attractive, bright-white color consumers love so much, of course. The charred bone absorbs color from liquefied sugarcane crystals—a process patented by Louis Constant in 1812—leaving the sugar stripped of color and, eventually, of flavor, as the natural molasses will be removed before refining is completed. The liquefied sugarcane is broken back into crystals in a vacuum, and the molasses is separated by centrifuge.

Processed brown sugar isn't any better. During the first steps of refining, the outer hulls of the sugarcane crystals are removed. After all the bone char filtering and molasses removal, those hulls are simply added back in to create brown sugar.

Sugar beets are another source of commercial sugar, and not refined with bone char. However, genetic modification of sugar beets has become very common in production, with one source citing that by the 2010 growing season, ninety-five percent of sugar beet acres in the United States were planted with genetically modified sugar-beet seed. While a U.S. District Court judge revoked the genetically modified sugar beets' deregulation in August 2010, appeals from interested parties—including the company that engineered the GMO sugar beets and a seed company—insisted that revocation of the deregulation would cause a sugar shortage. In February 2011, an announcement proclaimed that the GMO sugar beets had been "partially deregulated," pending the outcome of an Environmental Impact Study, and farmers would be allowed to continue planting the modified sugar beet crops. (http://en.wikipedia.org/wiki/Sugar_beet)

So, what's a conscientious vegan to do?

Much like Christina-Marie, her sweetener is less than completely refined. She uses cane juice crystals in place of white sugar and brown sugar, and she doesn't adjust the measure. She simply substitutes teaspoon for teaspoon, cup for cup. In fact, the less refined your sugar, the more flavor your foods will contain. When searching for a sugar product free of bone char processing or GMOs, look for the following types of labeling, experiment with a few, and select your favorite:

Cane juice crystals or cane juice
Turbinado sugar
Raw sugar
Organic sugar
Demerara sugar
Muscovado sugar
Date sugar (though date sugar can be expensive, and does not melt or dissolve like crystallized cane sugar)

When a recipe calls for powdered sugar, remember that standard powdered or confectioner's sugar is simply white refined sugar, pulverized into powder, with cornstarch or some other anti-clumping ingredient added.

Opting for a powdered sugar labeled "organic" will ensure you're using a vegan-friendly product.

CHAPTER EIGHT: WHAT ABOUT HONEY?

Christina-Marie is always amused when someone asks her about the vegan diet, listens to her answer explaining that no animal products are consumed by those following a vegan diet, and. then—invariably—asks, "What about honey?"

Is honey production really such a little-understood mystery? Did no one else read Winnie the Pooh stories as a child?

No, no, no—a hundred thousand times, no. Honey is not vegan. It is produced by bees, just as eggs are produced by birds. Vegans don't eat honey.

However, vegans have been known affectionately to refer to their friends who eschew all animal products EXCEPT honey as "*bee*gans."

COOKIES AND BISCOTTI

Peanut Butter Oatmeal Chocolate Chip Cookies

1¼ c. unbleached flour
1 c. oatmeal
1 t. salt
1 t. baking soda
1½ c. cane juice crystals or natural sugar
½ c. dairy-free margarine
½ c. creamy or chunky peanut butter
1 t. vanilla extract
1 T. egg replacer powder, beaten with 4 T. warm water
1 package dairy-free chocolate chips

Preheat oven to 375 degrees.

In a medium bowl, combine flour, oats, salt and baking soda.

In a large bowl, cream together the cane juice crystals or sugar, margarine, peanut butter, vanilla extract, and prepared egg replacer.

Add oat and flour mixture to creamed peanut butter

mixture in large bowl and stir until well-combined.

Add chocolate chips and mix until evenly distributed.

Grease baking sheets or cover with parchment paper and drop cookie dough by Tablespoons onto cookie sheet (we use a #50 scoop), about 2" apart.

Bake for about 12 minutes, or until edges just begin to brown.

Allow to rest on cookie sheet for 2 minutes before transferring to cooling rack.

Makes about 48 cookies.

View photos and tutorial of this recipe online at: http://www.sexyveganmama.com/2011/11/recipe-peanut-butter-oatmeal-chocolate.html

Granny's Angelica Cookies

Christina-Marie found the recipe for her grandmother's cookies in her mom's recipe box. With a few minor alterations, she was able to veganize it. Granny has moved on from this life, but Christina-Marie is sure she wouldn't mind her granddaughter having ditched the butter. When Christina-Marie offers these cookies to friends, she always uses Granny's standard phrase (originally attributed to a baby brother)—"Take a lot... Take TWO!"

This is a melt-in-your-mouth cookie with a sugary

coating, and wonderful when served up with a cup of coffee or espresso. By all means, have two, at the very least.

1 c. vegan stick margarine
4 T. cane juice crystals or natural sugar
2 t. vanilla extract
2 c. pecans, finely ground
2 c. unbleached flour
Organic powdered sugar for rolling

Preheat oven to 300 degrees.

Cream together margarine and cane juice crystals or sugar until light and fluffy.

Blend in vanilla and ground pecans.

Add flour and mix well.

Roll dough into balls about the size of walnuts and place on lightly greased baking sheet, about one inch apart.

Bake for 20 minutes. Cookies will be slightly dry on the outside, and firm to the touch.

Cool slightly.

Roll in powdered sugar while still warm.

Let cool completely and enjoy.

Makes approximately 36 cookies, depending on how big you define "walnut size"

Kahlua® Crinkle Cookies

Chocolate crinkle cookies are a childhood favorite of Christina-Marie, and she hadn't had them in years so she set out to create a vegan recipe she could make and share with friends. And, you know, a little booze couldn't hurt in dealing with those childhood memories, right? The result? Kahlua® Crinkle Cookies! They have just a touch of coffee flavor, and they're delicious!

1 c. unsweetened cocoa powder
2 c. cane juice crystals or natural sugar
½ c. oil
2 T. Ener-G egg replacer, beaten with 6 T. warm water
2 t. Kahlua® or coffee flavoring
2 c. unbleached flour
2 t. baking powder
½ t. salt
4 T. water
1 c. organic powdered or confectioner's sugar, set aside

In a large mixing bowl, combine cocoa powder, sugar and oil, mashing out any lumps and ensuring oil is evenly distributed.

Put cocoa mixture in microwave for 30 seconds, stir, microwave for another minute and stir thoroughly.

Add egg replacer and Kahlua®, then whip with a wire whisk or beater.

In a separate large bowl, combine flour, baking powder and salt, mixing well.

Add cocoa mixture to flour mixture, stirring until well mixed.

Add water, a Tablespoon at a time, and blend in to moisten dough.

Cover dough with plastic wrap or put in a large zipper bag, then chill in refrigerator for four hours.

Preheat oven to 350 degrees.

Use a rounded teaspoon to scoop dough, then roll into balls, about 1¼" in diameter.

Coat balls completely in confectioner's sugar, then place on a lightly oiled baking sheet, flattening gently with the heel of your hand.

Bake for 10 minutes and allow to cool for 5 minutes before removing from baking sheet.

Makes about 60 dainty cookies.

View photos and tutorial of this recipe online at:

http://www.sexyveganmama.com/2010/12/sexy-vegan-mama-kahlua-crinkle-cookies.html

Coconut Florentines

Food-as-art is not everyone's gift. We're here to tell you, these cookies taste exactly the same if the chocolate is drizzled in an "I don't give a _ _" manner, rather than a lacy pattern.

½ c. unbleached flour
¼ t. baking soda
⅛ t. salt
¼ c. vegan stick margarine
⅓ c. cane juice crystals or natural sugar
2 T. light corn syrup
½ T. egg replacer, beaten with 2 T. water
½ c. flaked coconut
½ t. vanilla extract
¼ c. non-dairy chocolate chips
1 T. vegan stick margarine

Preheat oven to 350 degrees.

Stir flour with baking soda and salt.

Cream in margarine.

Gradually beat in cane juice crystals or sugar, and continue beating until light and fluffy.

Add corn syrup and egg replacer, blending well.

Stir in flour mixture, coconut, and vanilla.

Drop by half-teaspoonfuls onto greased baking sheets, about two inches apart.

Bake about 10 minutes. Remove baking sheets from oven and cool 1 minute, then quickly remove wafers from baking sheets. If wafers harden on pan, return to oven for a few minutes.

Melt chocolate and 1 Tablespoon margarine in saucepan over very low heat, stirring constantly. Drizzle in a lacy pattern over the wafers. Let stand until chocolate is firm.

Frangelico® Shortbread Cookies

Christina-Marie has been terrified of shortbread ever since her pastor replaced their communion wafers with shortbread, causing Christina-Marie to panic and spit out the "body of Christ." This shortbread, though, Christina-Marie would gladly accept as a sacrament stand-in.

These cookies are crisp and crunchy and hold their shape well. They are also delightful with Gran Marnier® or orange flavoring instead of Frangelico®. Pay careful attention to these cookies as they bake. Timing is everything! If the cookies bake too long, the liqueur will scorch—and then you'll cry in frustration.

1½ c. vegan stick margarine
1 cup cane juice crystals or natural sugar
1 t. Frangelico® or hazelnut flavoring
3½ c. unbleached flour
¼ t. salt
½ c. slivered almonds, coarsely chopped.

In a large bowl, cream together margarine and cane juice crystals or sugar.

Add Frangelico® or flavoring and mix thoroughly.

In a small bowl, combine flour, salt and almonds, then add to margarine mixture, stirring *and stirring* some more, until all the flour is blended in. If the dough is too dry, you can add 1 or 2 teaspoons of water.

Gather dough into a ball, flatten into a thick circle, and cover with plastic wrap or put into a large plastic zipper bag, then refrigerate for an hour.

Preheat oven to 350 degrees.

Remove dough from refrigerator and roll out to ½" thickness.

Cut into shapes and bake on a lightly oiled baking sheet for 10 to 13 minutes.

Remove cookies from the oven when they first start to slightly brown around the edges.

Let cookies cool on baking sheet for about 5 minutes before transferring to a cooling rack.

The number of cookies this recipe yields will depend on the size the dough is cut into.

See photos of this recipe online at:

http://www.sexyveganmama.com/2010/12/sexy-vegan-mama-frangelico-shortbread.html

Amaretto Sugar Cookies

For all of the crazy mad skills of Mr. Wright, Christina-Marie's husband, one thing he is not is a baker. Perhaps that's why, when he used the last of Christina-Marie's vanilla extract while he was making pancakes, one Sunday morning, he didn't put "Run to store immediately to buy more vanilla before Mama tries to bake something and turns into a vegan Betty Crocker in a homicidal rage" at the top of his priorities.

That's how Christina-Marie ended up improvising this recipe for Amaretto Sugar Cookies. (It should come as no surprise that—although her pantry may not be inventoried—Sexy Vegan Mama's liquor cabinet is meticulously attended and regularly replenished.)

Please be aware, your arm will get very tired creaming and stirring, so we recommend taking a couple swigs of the amaretto right off the bat, before you begin mixing.

¾ c. vegan stick margarine, chilled/firm
1 c. cane juice crystals or natural sugar
1 T. egg replacer powder, prepared with 4 T. warm water and mixed well (or another equivalent of 2 eggs)
1 t. amaretto
2½ c. unbleached flour
1 t. baking powder
1 t. salt

Topping:

⅓-½ c. cane juice crystals or natural sugar
2 T. ground cinnamon

(Optional: You may omit the cinnamon and use candy sprinkles, or make your own colored natural sugar sprinkles, if you're really ambitious. Mix organic coarse sugar with food coloring. Spread out on waxed paper and dry well. Wear gloves.)

In a large bowl, cream together the margarine and cane juice crystals or sugar. Make sure no lumps of margarine remain.

Add prepared egg replacer and amaretto and mix thoroughly.

Add in flour, baking powder and salt, stirring until well-blended.

Gather dough into a ball, cover with plastic wrap or put into a large plastic zipper bag, and then put it in the refrigerator to chill for 1–2 hours.

Remove dough and preheat oven to 350 degrees.

Roll dough out to about ¼" thick with a rolling pin, then use cookie cutters to shape.

Carefully transfer cut cookies onto a lightly-oiled baking sheet, sprinkle with topping, and bake for 8 to 10 minutes, or until edges just begin to brown slightly.

Allow cookies to rest on baking sheet about 10 minutes, then transfer to a cooling rack.

You may opt to frost the cookies after baking. In this case, omit sprinkled topping before baking.

The number of cookies this recipe yields will depend on the size of your cookie cutters.

See photos of this recipe online at:

http://www.sexyveganmama.com/2010/12/sexy-vegan-mama-amaretto-sugar-cookies.html

Chinese Almond Cookies

1 c. cane juice crystals or natural sugar
1½ c. vegan stick margarine
3 c. unbleached flour

¼ t. baking soda
½ t. salt
1 t. almond extract
½ T. egg replacer, beaten with 2 T. water
½ c. finely chopped almonds
Red food color or whole raw almonds for decoration

Preheat oven to 350 degrees.

Cream together cane juice crystals or natural sugar and margarine.

Add flour, baking soda and salt.

Mix in extract, egg replacer, and almonds.

Shape into 1½" balls and flatten slightly.

Dot center of cookie with small cork dipped in red food-coloring, or place a whole raw almond in the center of each cookie.

Bake for 10 to 12 minutes or until lightly browned. Cool a few minutes before removing from baking sheet.

Makes approximately four dozen cookies.

Chocolate-Frosted Coconut Cookies

¼ c. vegan stick margarine
¾ c. cane juice crystals or natural sugar
1 T. egg replacer powder, beaten with 4 T. water
½ c. vegan sour cream
½ t. vanilla extract
¼ t. baking soda
¼ t. baking powder
¼ t. salt
1⅓ c. unbleached flour
1 c. flaked coconut

Chocolate Icing:

1 T. vegan stick margarine
⅛ c. non-dairy chocolate chips
3 T. soy milk
Dash salt
½ t. vanilla extract
1½ c. organic powdered sugar

Preheat oven to 400 degrees.

Cream margarine with cane juice crystals or sugar until blended.

Add "eggs" and mix well.

Stir in sour cream, vanilla, baking soda, baking powder and salt.

Add flour and coconut. Mix until a stiff dough forms.

Drop by rounded spoonfuls onto a lightly greased cookie sheet.

Bake for 8 to 10 minutes, or until cookies are golden around the edges and firm to the touch.

Frost while hot with chocolate icing.

Icing Directions:

Place margarine and chocolate chips in top part of double boiler. Melt together over hot, not boiling, water.

Stir in soy milk, salt, vanilla and powdered sugar.

Mix until a glossy, spreadable icing forms. If necessary, add 1 to 2 teaspoons more soy milk.

Makes approximately 36 cookies.

Cocoa Biscotti

Biscotti, with a long and glorious history that dates back centuries to the Italian city of Prato, are traditionally comprised of flour, eggs, sugar and almonds. Modern adaptations often add baking powder, spices, dried fruits and a wide variety of nuts.

Due to their dry, hard composition, biscotti are best served with a beverage—frequently in the United States with espresso, coffee drinks or tea. In some European countries, biscotti are served with wine, such as vin santo *or* muscat.

1 c. unbleached flour
½ c. cane juice crystals or natural sugar
1 t. baking powder
⅓ c. unsweetened cocoa powder
½ t. salt
¼ c. nuts of your choice (optional)
1 T. egg replacer powder, mixed with ¼ c. water
1 T. flavoring or liqueur of your choice

Preheat oven to 350 degrees.

In a large bowl, stir together flour, cane juice crystals or sugar, baking powder, cocoa powder, salt and optional nuts.

In a small bowl, combine prepared egg replacer and flavoring or liqueur.

Pour liquid mixture into dry ingredients and stir until dry ingredients are thoroughly moistened and mixed in. The resulting dough should be sticky and a bit shiny. You may need to add more water or flour to achieve the right consistency.

Gather the dough into a ball and place on an oiled baking sheet. Roll the ball into two flattened "logs," each about 2" wide, ½" high and 12" long.

Bake logs for 25 minutes, and then remove from oven.

Reduce oven temperature to 300 degrees.

Allow biscuits to cool for 10 minutes, then slice the logs diagonally into biscuits about ½" wide.

Place biscuits, sliced side down, on baking sheet and bake for 10 minutes.

Flip biscuits over and bake for an additional 10 minutes.

Allow to cool completely before storing.

View photos and tutorial of this recipe online at:

http://www.sexyveganmama.com/2011/09/cocoa-biscotti-with-pics-by-mad-rooster.html

CHEESECAKES AND TORTES

Peanut Butter S'mores Cheesecake

This cheesecake has a very thick graham crust, a layer of chocolate cheesecake, a layer of peanut butter cheesecake, and a layer of traditional vanilla cheesecake.

The first bites were bliss. Our seconds were ecstasy-inducing. By our third sweet, rich bites, we realized we actually wouldn't mind dying at that very moment, except it would mean we wouldn't get to finish our slices. We hope you find the results of this recipe as equally gasp-worthy as we did.

Crust Ingredients:

1 - 14.4 oz. package graham crackers (check for honey and dairy)
½ c. dairy-free margarine, melted

Filling Ingredients:

1 - 14 oz. package firm tofu (not silken)

½ c. soy milk

1 - 8 oz. package vegan cream cheese

¾ c. cane juice crystals or natural sugar

3 T. egg replacer powder (do NOT beat with water)

2 T. lemon juice

½ T. vanilla extract

1 c. dairy-free chocolate chips, melted (melt on stovetop or in microwave, stirring every 30 seconds)

½ c. smooth peanut butter (tip: spray measuring cup with nonstick spray before filling)

Dairy-free chocolate chips and chocolate syrup (for garnish)

Crust Directions:

Preheat oven to 325 degrees.

Use a food processor or blender to whiz the graham crackers into fine crumbs.

Add melted margarine and stir thoroughly.

Press mixture into bottom of lightly-oiled 9" springform pan. Tip: Cut a circle of parchment or waxed paper slightly smaller than bottom of pan and line for easy removal from pan.

Bake for 5 minutes and remove from oven. Set aside.

Filling Directions:

Put tofu and soy milk into a large blender pitcher or food processor and blend until creamy.

Add cream cheese and blend until smooth.

Add cane juice crystals or sugar, egg replacer powder, lemon juice and vanilla. Blend until sugar crystals are dissolved.

Set aside 2 cups of filling, separated.

For chocolate layer, combine melted chocolate chips with one cup of reserved cheesecake filling, mixing until smooth. Pour over graham cracker crust and evenly spread.

Refrigerate crust and first layer for 30 minutes to "set" the layer.

For peanut butter layer, combine peanut butter with one remaining cup of cheesecake filling, mixing until smooth.

Pour and spread over chocolate layer.

Refrigerate crust and first two layers for 30 minutes to "set" layers.

Spread remaining filling over top of peanut butter layer.

Heat oven to 350 degrees.

Wrap bottom of spring-form pan with several layers of foil.

Set wrapped spring-form into bottom of a deep, larger baking pan and fill with boiling water. This water bath will bake the cheesecake from the sides and result in more even cooking.

Use hot pads to put the larger pan filled with boiling water and spring form into the oven. Please be careful!

Bake until cheesecake begins to pull away from edges of pan—about 55 to 60 minutes. Don't let it brown.

CAREFULLY remove pan from oven.

Let stand for 15 minutes, then carefully remove spring-form from larger pan and peel away foil. Chill for 2 or more hours before serving. The longer, the better.

Garnish with chocolate chips and drizzle with chocolate syrup before serving.

See photos and tutorial of this recipe online at:

http://www.sexyveganmama.com/2011/01/recipe-vegan-peanut-butter-smores.html

Blueberry Citrus Cheesecake with Oat Crust

We adore the combination of blueberries and citrus fruits. It's a wonderful marriage of flavors, and the contrast of sharp oranges and yellows against the blue-purple of the berries is exciting. This cheesecake consummates the union of a thin, luscious layer of orange cheesecake stacked atop a thick, creamy layer of blueberry cheesecake and a thick oat crust.

Crust Ingredients:

1 c. unbleached or whole wheat flour
1 c. oats, finely ground in a blender or food processor
½ c. cane juice crystals or natural sugar
1 c. vegan stick margarine

Filling Ingredients:

1 - 14 oz. package firm or extra firm tofu (not silken)
½ c. vegan soy yogurt (plain or vanilla)
1 Tablespoon lemon juice
¼ c. frozen orange juice concentrate, thawed
1 – 8 oz. tub vegan cream cheese
⅛ c. egg replacer powder (do NOT mix with water)
1 c. cane juice crystals or natural sugar
½ c. fresh or frozen blueberries (thaw first if frozen)

OPTIONAL: 1 T. fresh orange zest

Crust Directions:

Preheat oven to 350 degrees.

In a medium bowl, mix flour, oats, and cane juice crystals or sugar.

Add stick margarine and mix with a fork or pastry blender. until crumbly.

Press mixture into bottom of lightly-oiled 9" springform pan. Tip: Cut a circle of parchment or waxed paper slightly smaller than bottom of pan and line for easy removal from pan.

Use a fork to make small holes throughout the crust.

Bake for 15 minutes, remove from oven, and let cool completely.

Filling Directions:

Put tofu, yogurt, lemon juice, and orange juice into a large blender pitcher or food processor and blend until creamy.

Add cream cheese and blend until smooth.

Add cane juice crystals or sugar and egg replacer powder. Blend until sugar crystals are dissolved.

Remove approximately one-third of filling. Add orange

zest, if desired, and mix well. Set aside.

Using a blender or food processor, chop blueberries and gently fold into remaining two-thirds of filling. Don't over-mix, or your cheesecake will come out more gray-colored than blue-purple.

Pour blueberry filling over baked oat crust and spread evenly.

Refrigerate the crust and first layer for 30 minutes to "set" layer.

Pour orange layer over blueberry layer and spread evenly.

Heat oven to 350 degrees.

Wrap bottom of spring-form pan with several layers of foil.

Set wrapped spring-form into bottom of a deep, larger baking pan and fill with boiling water. This water bath will bake the cheesecake from the sides and result in more even cooking.

Use hot pads to put the larger pan filled with boiling water and spring form into the oven. Please be careful!

Bake until cheesecake begins to pull away from edges of pan—about 55 to 60 minutes. Don't let it brown.

CAREFULLY remove pan from oven.

Let stand for 15 minutes, then carefully remove springform from larger pan and peel away foil. Chill for 2 or more hours before serving. The longer, the better.

Garnish with orange or tangerine slices and blueberries.

See photos and tutorial of this recipe online at:

http://www.sexyveganmama.com/2011/05/recipe-vegan-blueberry-citrus.html

Chocolate Mint Cheesecake

"A grasshopper walks into a bar and hops up onto the counter. The bartender says, 'We have a drink named after you.' The grasshopper replies 'You have a drink named Irving?'"

Crust Ingredients:

36 graham cracker squares (⅔ of a 14.4-oz. box; check for honey and dairy)
½ c. vegan stick margarine, melted
3 T. cocoa powder

Filling Ingredients:

1 - 14 oz. package firm tofu, drained (not silken)
½ c. vanilla or plain soy yogurt

- ¼ c. peppermint schnapps or Crème de Menthe (white or green)
- ½ T. peppermint extract
- 1 - 8 oz. tub vegan cream cheese
- ¾ c. cane juice crystals or natural sugar
- 3 T. egg replacer powder (do NOT mix with water)
- 1 T. fresh peppermint leaves, milled or finely chopped
- OPTIONAL: A few drops of green food color
- 1 c. dairy-free chocolate chips, melted (melt on stovetop or in microwave, stirring every 30 seconds)
- Dairy-free chocolate chips, mint sprigs and chocolate syrup *(for garnish)*

Crust Directions:

Preheat oven to 325 degrees.

Use a food processor or blender to whiz the graham crackers into fine crumbs.

Add cocoa powder and melted margarine, stirring thoroughly.

Press mixture into bottom of lightly-oiled 9" springform pan. Tip: Cut a circle of parchment or waxed paper slightly smaller than bottom of pan and line for easy removal from pan.

Bake for 5 minutes, and remove from oven. Set aside.

Filling Directions:

Put tofu, yogurt, schnapps or Crème de menthe, and peppermint extract into a large blender pitcher or food processor and blend until creamy.

Add cream cheese and blend until smooth.

Add cane juice crystals or sugar, egg replacer powder and peppermint leaves.

Blend until sugar crystals are dissolved. You'll have about three cups of filling.

Remove 2 cups of filling. For mint layers, combine food coloring (if desired) with those 2 cups of cheesecake filling, mixing until smooth.

Pour and spread 1 cup of mint filling over chocolate crust. Set aside the remaining cup of mint filling.

Refrigerate crust and first layer for 30 minutes to "set" the layer.

For chocolate layer, combine melted chocolate chips with one cup remaining cheesecake filling, mixing until smooth. Pour over first mint layer and spread evenly.

Refrigerate crust and layers for 30 minutes to "set" the layers.

Pour the remaining mint filling over the chocolate layer, spreading evenly.

Heat oven to 350 degrees.

Wrap bottom of spring-form pan with several layers of foil.

Set wrapped spring-form into bottom of a deep, larger baking pan and fill with boiling water. This water bath will bake the cheesecake from the sides and result in more even cooking.

Use hot pads to put the larger pan filled with boiling water and spring form into the oven. Please be careful!

Bake until cheesecake begins to pull away from edges of pan—about 55 to 60 minutes. Don't let it brown.

CAREFULLY remove pan from oven.

Let stand for 15 minutes, then carefully remove spring-form from larger pan and peel away foil. Chill for at least 2 hours before serving. The longer, the better.

Garnish with chocolate chips and mint sprigs (optional), drizzling with chocolate syrup before serving.

See photos and tutorial of this recipe online at:

http://www.sexyveganmama.com/2011/05/recipe-vegan-chocolate-mint-cheesecake.html

Caramel Chocolate Almond Truffle Torte

Know what's great about recipes? You don't have to follow them. You can give them your own flavor, modify them to suit what's in your pantry, or just use them as inspiration. This one is an adaptation of Vegangela's Chocolate Truffle Torte. Check out her fantastic recipes at http://www.vegangela.com.

Crust Ingredients:

1 c. unbleached or whole wheat flour
1 c. oats, finely ground in a blender or food processor
½ c. cane juice crystals or natural sugar
1 c. vegan stick margarine

Caramel Truffle Layer Ingredients:

1 c. cane juice crystals or natural sugar
½ c. vegan stick margarine
1 t. vanilla
1 t. cornstarch
½ c. slivered almonds

Chocolate Truffle Layer Ingredients:

16 oz. dairy-free chocolate chips
½ c. soy milk
½ c. vegan stick margarine
½ c. slivered almonds, finely chopped

Crust Directions:

Preheat oven to 350 degrees.

In a medium bowl, mix flour, oats, and cane juice crystals or sugar.

Add stick margarine and mix with a fork or pastry blender until crumbly.

Press mixture firmly and evenly into the bottom of a 9" spring form pan.

Use a fork to make small holes throughout the crust, to help it bake evenly.

Bake for 15 minutes, then let cool completely.

Caramel Truffle Layer Directions:

Melt margarine in a small saucepan.

Stir in cane juice crystals or sugar and vanilla, stirring constantly, until the mixture is smooth and thoroughly melted.

Add cornstarch and stir until it is evenly distributed and the sauce is shiny.

Pour caramel over cooled crust. Sprinkle almonds in an even layer over the caramel sauce.

Refrigerate for half an hour, or until caramel thickens.

Chocolate Truffle Layer Directions:

Bring a medium pot of water to boil, and turn down to a simmer.

Place the margarine and chocolate in a stainless steel or glass mixing bowl, then place bowl over simmering water and stir until chocolate is melted.

Stir in soy milk until smooth.

Pour chocolate mixture over caramel layer, using a spiral motion, working inward, so as not to disturb the nuts too much. Tap the bottom of pan on counter to settle the chocolate of any air bubbles.

Refrigerate for 15 minutes, and then sprinkle the chopped nuts on top.

Return to fridge for another 2 hours.

As Vegangela noted, this dessert is incredibly rich, and best served in dainty wedges.

See photos and tutorial of this recipe online at:

http://www.sexyveganmama.com/2011/02/chocolate-almond-truffle-torte.html

CAKES, CUPCAKES, BROWNIES AND FROSTINGS

Double Chocolate Chai Cake

1⅔ c. unbleached flour
1 c. cane juice crystals or natural sugar
¼ c. cocoa powder
1 t. baking soda
½ t. salt
1½ t. loose chai tea
1 c. water
⅓ c. oil
1 t. apple cider vinegar
1 t. vanilla
½ c. dairy-free chocolate chips

Preheat oven to 350 degrees.

In a large mixing bowl, combine dry ingredients and mix.

Add wet ingredients and beat on high with mixer for 2

minutes or beat 150 strokes by hand.

Pour into greased 8" or 9" round cake pan. Note: I cut a circle of wax paper and place it in the bottom of the pan to help it come out of the pan easily. I highly recommend you do so, too. This recipe doesn't have any eggs to bind it, so the wax paper helps the bottom of the cake stay together when it's warm.

Sprinkle chocolate chips over top of batter before placing in oven.

Bake for 35 to 40 minutes, or until the cake begins to pull away from the sides of the pan and a toothpick inserted into the middle of the cake comes out clean.

Let cool in pan for 15 minutes, and then turn out onto a cooling rack. Wait another 15 minutes, and then turn right-side up onto a serving plate.

This sweet cake needs no frosting, but you may dust with organic powdered sugar, if desired.

This recipe makes one tall, decadent round.

Derby Gurlz Double Mocha Mini-Cupcakes

These frosted mini chocolate treasures are named for the Apple City Roller Derby girls, who were brave enough to be our taste testers. For the record, Christina-Marie is a derby-girl dropout, but that's just how she rolls. Get it? "Roll?" Roller derby? Ha!

1⅔ c. unbleached flour
1 c. cane juice crystals or natural sugar
¼ c. cocoa powder
1 t. baking soda
½ t. salt
1 c. cold strong coffee or espresso
⅓ c. oil
1 t. apple cider vinegar
½ t. vanilla extract
1 c. non-dairy chocolate chips

Preheat oven to 350 degrees.

In a large bowl, combine flour, cane juice crystals or sugar, cocoa powder, baking soda and salt. Stir together until well-mixed.

Add coffee, oil, vinegar and vanilla and stir until smooth and blended.

Line a mini-cupcake baking tin with mini-cupcake papers. Tip: Spray the cupcake papers with non-stick spray before putting batter in. The cupcakes won't stick to the paper.

Fill the cups about ⅔ full, and drop a few non-dairy chocolate chips on top. We think 4 or 5 is adequate, but Christina-Marie's youngest daughter, "Snugglebug," thinks about 10 is better.

Bake for about 15 minutes, or until a toothpick inserted straight down into the middle comes out clean.

This recipe makes about 48 mini-cupcakes.

Allow to cool completely before frosting. While waiting, make your frosting. Recommended: Coconut Almond Cream Cheese Frosting (see very next recipe)

Frost your mini-cupcakes, dust with cocoa powder and top with a chocolate chip.

See photos and tutorial of this recipe online at:

http://www.sexyveganmama.com/2011/01/recipe-derby-gurlz-double-mocha-mini.html

Coconut Almond Cream Cheese Frosting

While Christina-Marie and I love our stand mixers, you can make frosting by hand or with a hand mixer, if necessary. Just be sure to blend everything completely.

½ c. vegan stick margarine
4 oz. vegan cream cheese (half an 8-ounce tub)
2 t. almond extract
⅛ c. full-fat coconut milk (shake/mix well before measuring)
About 6 c. organic powdered sugar

Cream together margarine and cream cheese.

Add almond extract and coconut milk and cream again.

At this point, the mixture may begin to look grainy. That's fine. It's just the alcohol in the extract separating from the oils in the cream cheese and margarine, and the effect will disappear when you add the sugar.

Add powdered sugar, one cup at a time, blending in until smooth. You may use more or less powdered sugar, depending on how thick you want your frosting. We pipe ours from decorating bags, so we like it a little stiffer. If you're just spreading the frosting on the cupcakes, you can use less sugar for a softer, smoother frosting.

Clementine Mini-Cupcakes

These cupcakes were originally created for Christina-Marie's local writers' group, the Rebel Writers, and for Samuel Clemens, also known as Mark Twain, during the newsworthy "sanitized" release of his original work, THE ADVENTURES OF HUCKLEBERRY

FINN. *Publisher NewSouth Books announced plans to re-release the book, removing some of Clemens's original wording.*

Some thought the scrubbing of dated, racist language was appropriate. Others thought it was censorship, and obscured a historic view of the South.

As for Christina-Marie, she salutes Clemens/Twain as a rebel writer. That's why these mini-treats are also known as Rebel Writer Samuel Clemen(tine)s Mini-Cupcakes:

½ c. vegan stick margarine
1⅓ c. cane juice crystals or natural sugar
3 c. unbleached flour
1 T. baking powder
½ t. salt
1½ c. soy milk
½ c. Clementine juice (about 5 or 6 Clementines, juiced)
¼ c. plus 2 T. raspberry purée (about 1 cup raspberries, blended)[1]
1 t. vanilla

Preheat oven to 350 degrees.

Cream together margarine and cane juice crystals or sugar.

Add flour, baking powder and salt, and mix well.

---

[1]. Frozen raspberries may be used in this recipe. Simply thaw before blending.

Blend in soy milk, Clementine juice, raspberry purée and vanilla.

Line mini-cupcake tin with paper or foil liners. Tip: Spray liners with a bit of non-stick cooking spray before filling to prevent the cupcakes from sticking.

Fill cups ⅔ full with batter.

Bake for 15 minutes, or until a toothpick inserted into the middle of the center cupcake comes out clean.

Allow to cool completely before frosting. Recommended: Clementine Sour Cream Frosting (see recipe that directly follows)

Frost mini-cupcakes, and garnish with Clementine zest, if desired.

See photos and tutorial of this recipe online at:

http://www.sexyveganmama.com/2011/02/rebel-writer-samuel-clementines-mini.html

Clementine Sour Cream Frosting

We love our stand mixers, but you can make frosting by hand or with a hand mixer, if necessary. Just be sure to blend everything completely.

½ c. vegan stick margarine
⅓ c. vegan sour cream

¼ c. Clementine juice (about 2 or 3 Clementines, juiced)
5 to 6 c. organic powdered sugar

Blend margarine and sour cream together.

Add Clementine juice and beat until smooth.

Add powdered sugar, 1 cup at a time, blending in until smooth. You may use more or less powdered sugar, depending on how thick you want your frosting. We pipe ours from decorating bags, so we like it a little stiffer. If you're just spreading the frosting on the cupcakes, you can use less sugar for a softer, smoother frosting.

Pineapple RUM-side Down Cake

Pineapple and rum were made for one another, and cake is good. Cake is GREAT when it's made with pineapple and dark rum, a marriage inspired by Christina-Marie's new love affair with the pineapple-flavored rum she picked up in the Bahamas, and a long-standing affair with dark rum in general.
  Here's how the hook-up went down:

1½ c. unbleached flour
1 c. cane juice crystals or natural sugar
½ t. salt
1 t. baking soda
⅓ c. oil

1 T. apple cider vinegar
½ c. pineapple juice (drained from can of pineapple, below)
½ c. dark rum
1 c. cane juice crystals or natural sugar
1 t. dark rum
1 - 20 oz. can pineapple rings in own juice (not syrup)

Preheat oven to 350 degrees.

In a large bowl, combine flour, first cup cane juice crystals or sugar, baking soda and salt.

In a medium bowl, stir together oil, cider vinegar, pineapple juice and ½ cup dark rum.

In a small bowl, mix additional cane juice crystals or sugar with 1 teaspoon dark rum until all sugar crystals are coated, and mixture resembles light brown sugar.

Oil a 10" spring form pan and arrange pineapple rings in bottom of pan. Tip: For easier removal from pan, a sheet of waxed paper may be cut to fit in bottom of spring form and inserted before arranging pineapple rings.

Sprinkle sugar and rum mixture over pineapple rings.

Pour liquid ingredients into dry ingredients and beat vigorously by hand or electric mixer to remove lumps from batter.

Pour batter over pineapple slices and bake for 35 minutes or until top is golden brown, cake begins to pull away from sides of pan, and a toothpick inserted into the middle of the cake comes out clean.

Remove from oven and allow to cool for 20 to 25 minutes before removing spring form ring.

Place an upside-down serving plate on top of cake, turn right side-up and remove spring form bottom (and waxed paper sheet, if used).

Allow to cool completely before slicing.

View photos and tutorial of this recipe online at:

http://www.sexyveganmama.com/2011/09/pineapple-rum-side-down-cake.html

Raspberry Cream Cheese Brownie Bites

These brownie bites, created in a mini-cupcake pan, are filled with a burst of sweet raspberry and cream cheese filling. For easy removal from the cupcake liners, spray each liner with non-stick cooking spray before filling. This recipe makes approximately 72 brownie bites.

2 c. frozen raspberries
1 c. cane juice crystals or natural sugar
4 T. cornstarch
½ c. cold water

2 c. unbleached flour
2 c. cane juice crystals or natural sugar
¾ c. cocoa powder
1 t. baking powder
1 t. salt
1 c. water
1 c. oil
1 t. vanilla
1 c. vegan cream cheese

Use the back of a spoon to break up raspberries into small chunks and put them in a medium saucepan.

Put cornstarch in a small bowl and gradually add water, stirring until smooth. Set aside.

Sprinkle cane juice crystals over raspberry chunks and heat over medium heat, stirring until cane juice crystals melt. The berries will begin to juice as the crystals dissolve, creating a berry syrup.

Gently increase heat to high. When syrup begins boiling, slowly pour in cornstarch mixture, stirring constantly. Boil until filling thickens—about 1 to 2 minutes. Remove from heat and allow to cool.

Preheat oven to 350 degrees.

In a large bowl, combine dry ingredients.

Add water and stir, wetting all ingredients.

Add oil and vanilla, mixing well.

Place a paper mini-cupcake liner in each cup of your pan. Fill each cup ½ with brownie mix.

Using a small spoon or a pastry bag without a decorating tip, add a dollop of raspberry filling—about the width of a quarter—to the top of each cup.

Again, using a small spoon or pastry bag—with a tip this time—add a grape-sized dollop of cream cheese. The raspberry filling may sink into the brownie mix a bit as you add the cream cheese. That's fine. In fact, it's perfect!

Bake 16 to 18 minutes.

View photos and tutorial of this recipe online at:

http://www.sexyveganmama.com/2011/01/recipe-vegan-raspberry-cream-cheese.html

William Maltese Spice Cake

Says Christina-Marie: "My esteemed co-author already has a spice blend (William Maltese Hottie Spice) named after him, so... Why not a spice cake? Many spice cake recipes call for raisins, but I prefer the tartness of cranberries. This, by the way, is not to imply Mr. Maltese is a 'tart' of any sort."

1¾ c. unbleached flour
1 c. cane juice crystals or natural sugar
½ t. baking soda
½ t. salt
1 t. cinnamon
½ t. nutmeg
½ t. ground cloves
1 c. dried cranberries
½ c. oil
1 T. vanilla extract
1 c. cold water
2 T. lemon juice

Preheat oven to 375 degrees.

Lightly grease an 8" or 9" cake pan.

In a large bowl, combine all dry ingredients and stir until mixture is silky and well-combined.

Mix in cranberries.

In a medium bowl, combine oil, vanilla and water.

Add contents of medium bowl to large bowl and stir well.

Add lemon juice to batter, stirring quickly, and then pour into baking pan. The cranberries will settle to the bottom of the pan, and will be on top when the cake is turned out of the pan.

Bake 35 to 45 minutes, or until cake begins to pull away from sides of pan and a toothpick inserted into center of cake comes out clean.

Allow to cool in pan for 10 minutes, and then turn cake out onto a serving plate. Allow to cool completely before slicing.

Serve as-is, dusted with organic powdered sugar or drizzle with a glaze made of water, organic powdered sugar and vanilla.

See photos of this recipe online at:

http://www.sexyveganmama.com/2012/05/maltese-vegan-spice-cake.html

PIES, PASTIES, AND CRISPS

Sexy Vegan Mama's Perfect Pie Crust

It's a learned skill, making the perfect pie crust, but it's really the key to making perfect pie. The authors learned the basics by watching their moms in their kitchens. Christina-Marie developed her vegan baking skills even more, later, as a young adult, working in her mother's bakery. It's not as hard as you might think to turn out a flaky, tasty crust without using butter.

To make two 10-inch pie crusts (if you have any dough left over, roll it out and cut it into squares, sprinkled with cane juice crystals and cinnamon for pie dough cookies):

1 c. vegan stick margarine
2⅔ c. unbleached flour
1 t. salt
7 to 8 T. cold water

In a large mixing bowl, combine flour and salt.

Cut margarine into flour mixture using a fork or pastry

blender. Knobby little pieces will form. Continue cutting margarine until "clumps" are about the size of petite peas.

Add water, 1 Tablespoon at a time, tossing with a fork until all the dough is moistened and sticks to itself more than it does the bowl. It may take more or less water than the recipe calls for.

Roll the dough into a ball and remove it from the bowl.

Divide the ball in half, forming 2 balls, and then flatten on a flour-covered cutting board.

Use a floured rolling pin on each flattened round to spread the dough into a 12" circle (13"-14" for deep-dish pans).

To transfer the crust into the pie pan, fold it carefully in fourths, place in the bottom of the pan, and then gently unfold it.

Using a knife or scissors, trim the crust to about ½ around the edge of the pan.

Tuck the excess edges under, forming a thick crust around the edge of the pie pan.

Using your thumb and forefingers, gently pinch the thick edge of the crust all the way around the rim of the pan, creating a fluted edge.

Use a fork to prick the bottom and sides of the crust to prevent puffing while baking.

If you are pre-baking your crust: Bake for 8 to 10 minutes in an oven preheated to 475 degrees.

If you are only making 1 pie or making crusts ahead of baking: Seal the unused, unbaked crust(s) in plastic wrap or a large zipper bag and store in the freezer. Crusts will keep up to 3 months if well-sealed. Let thaw completely before baking.

View photos and tutorial of this recipe online at:

http://www.sexyveganmama.com/2010/11/sexy-vegan-mama-perfect-pie-crust.html

Berry Mango Ginger Pie

Christina-Marie confesses: "Sometimes, I have strokes of genius that coincide with strokes of absentmindedness. The first time I made this pie, the flavors were exactly what I wanted, but it was too 'soupy.' I got feedback from a couple other bakers, and planned on making it again—except I didn't write down my original recipe attempt. Therefore, the next time, I had to re-create the recipe from memory, input, and a sprinkling of fabulous luck.

"I'm almost glad I forgot. The 'new' pie turned out even better than the original. Oh, and it tastes even better the next day, if you can keep yourself from

devouring it the very minute it comes out of the oven!"

- 4 c. mixed berries, fresh or partially thawed frozen berries, such as strawberries, blueberries, raspberries and blackberries
- 1 diced mango, peeled first
- 1 T. lemon juice
- ½ t. ginger powder
- ¼ c. "minute" tapioca
- ½ c. cane juice crystals or natural sugar

You'll also need:

One 9" unbaked pie crust, like Sexy Vegan Mama's Perfect Pie Crust, formed into a pie shell within a 9" pie pan.

Preheat oven to 425 degrees.

In a large bowl combine berries and mango.

Sprinkle in lemon juice and stir.

Add ginger, tapioca and cane juice crystals or sugar.

Mix well and allow to stand for 15 minutes.

Pour berry mixture into 9" unbaked pie crust shell.

Top with additional unbaked crust, joining and fluting edges. Slice vents into top crust, so steam and pressure can escape while the pie bakes. (Or, you may use an open-lattice design, if you so desire).

Cover edges of crust with a 2" to 3" strip of foil to prevent burning, and place pie on center rack in oven on baking sheet to catch spills.

Bake for 30 minutes.

Remove foil strips and bake for an additional 15 minutes to brown edges of crust.

Allow pie to cool almost completely before slicing, as the filling will continue to thicken after removal from oven.

View photos and tutorial of this recipe online at:

http://www.sexyveganmama.com/2011/09/recipe-vegan-berry-mango-ginger-pie.html

Très Riche Pecan Pie

Says Christina-Marie: "File this one under 'recipes developed under the influence of a very strong non-vegan craving.' It had literally been decades since I'd had pecan pie. Believe me, I was due."

    A southern favorite, pecan pie is usually made with corn syrup, butter and eggs and is rumored to have been developed by the French after settling in New Orleans—though attempts to trace the exact origins have proven inconclusive.

    "Veganizing" the recipe was no easy task, but

completely worth the trial and error. Enjoy!

1 c. cane juice crystals or natural sugar
3 T. quick tapioca
¼ c. soy milk or other non-dairy milk
1 T. egg replacer powder (do NOT mix with water)
½ c. vegan stick margarine, melted
1 T. vanilla
1½ c. shelled pecans

You'll also need:

One 9" unbaked pie crust, like Sexy Vegan Mama's Perfect Pie Crust, formed into a pie shell within a 9" pie pan.

Preheat oven to 375 degrees.

In a coffee grinder or blender, whiz the tapioca until finely powdered.

In a medium or large bowl, combine all ingredients, including powdered tapioca.

Stir until well-mixed and pour into unbaked pie crust.

Bake for 20 minutes.

Reduce oven temperature to 300 degrees and bake for 30 minutes longer.

Remove from oven and allow to cool before serving.

See photos of this recipe online at:

http://www.sexyveganmama.com/2011/09/vegan-pecan-pie-and-crimes-of-heart.html

Apple Peanut Butter Pie

Growing up in apple country, peanut butter on slices of crisp, freshly-picked apples was a favorite snack. This pie—adapted from a Christina-Marie family recipe—offers that classic combo between two flaky crusts.

4 large tart apples, like Granny Smiths
½ c. cane juice crystals or natural sugar
2 T. unbleached flour
½ t. cinnamon
¼ t. nutmeg
1 c. peanut butter

You'll also need:

One 9" unbaked pie crust, like Sexy Vegan Mama's Perfect Pie Crust, formed into a pie shell within a 9" pie pan.

Preheat oven to 425 degrees.

Peel, core, and thinly slice apples.

Mix together cane juice crystals or sugar, flour, cinnamon and nutmeg.

Toss this mixture together with the sliced apples in a large microwaveable bowl.

Cook apples in microwave until tender (approximately 6 to 8 minutes) stirring every 2 minutes.

Gently stir peanut butter into hot apple filling. Let filling cool to room temperature.

Spoon the cooled apple filling into the unbaked pie crust shell.

Cover with additional unbaked pie crust, and seal crust edges. Cut slits to allow steam to escape.

Bake at 425 degrees for 15 minutes.

Reduce oven temperature to 350 degrees and continue baking for an additional 25 to 35 minutes or until top crust is light golden brown.

Strawberry Banana Cream Pie with Chocolate Graham Crust

Strawberries and bananas just seem to go together. Add chocolate, and it's heavenly. How about a vegan banana cream pie with a berry twist, on a chocolate graham crust? Divine, right? Let's do it!

½ - 14.4 oz. package chocolate graham crackers (check for dairy and honey)
½ c. vegan stick margarine, melted

8 oz. fresh or frozen strawberries (thawed), sliced into ¼-inch slices
3 bananas, sliced into ¼-inch slices
2 T. lemon juice
Water enough to cover bananas
1 - 14-oz. block extra firm tofu (NOT silken), drained
1 T. vanilla
2 T. cornstarch
1 c. cane juice crystals or natural sugar

Preheat oven to 375 degrees.

In a blender or food processor, pulse the graham crackers into fine crumbs

Transfer chocolate graham crumbs to a medium-sized bowl.

Pour melted margarine over graham cracker crumbs and mix thoroughly.

Press crumb mixture into bottom of oiled 10-inch pie pan.

Line bottom of pie crust with strawberry slices. Set aside.

Place banana slices into a medium bowl.

Sprinkle in lemon juice, adding enough water to cover bananas.

Allow to soak for 10 minutes. This will help keep the bananas from browning as they bake.

Drain bananas.

In blender or food processor, puree bananas, tofu and vanilla.

In a small bowl, stir together cornstarch and cane juice crystals or sugar, then add to banana mixture in food processor or blender, and blend all until smooth.

Pour banana mixture into pie crust, over strawberries. The pie filling won't rise or expand during baking, so fill it right up to the top.

Bake for 30 to 35 minutes, or until top is a golden brown.

Remove from oven and allow to cool, and then refrigerate overnight. Slice and enjoy, with a dusting of cocoa powder, if desired.

See photos and tutorial of this recipe online at:

http://www.sexyveganmama.com/2011/08/vegan-strawberry-banana-cream-pie-with.html

Raspberry Lemonade Glacé Pie

We did mention this cookbook is not intended as a weight-loss guide, right?

Filling:

2 - 8 oz. tubs vegan cream cheese
1 c. cane juice crystals or natural sugar
1½ t. vanilla
¼ c. lemon juice
2 T. cornstarch

Topping:

½ c. cane juice crystals or natural sugar
1 T. cornstarch
½ c. water
1 c. chopped fresh or frozen raspberries, thawed
½ c. whole fresh or frozen raspberries, thawed

You'll also need:

One 9" unbaked pie crust, like Sexy Vegan Mama's Perfect Pie Crust, formed into a pie shell within a 9" pie pan.

Preheat oven to 350 degrees.

Combine filling ingredients in a blender or food processor.

Pour into unbaked pie crust pie shell and bake 45 to 50 minutes, or until top just begins to take on a golden hue, and the crust begins to brown.

Place baked pie on a cooling rack and allow to cool.

Prepare topping by combining cane juice crystals or sugar with cornstarch in a medium saucepan.

Gradually stir in water and chopped raspberries and cook over medium heat, stirring constantly, until mixture begins to thicken.

Bring to a boil and boil for 1 full minute while continuing to stir constantly to prevent burning.

Remove from heat.

Place whole raspberries evenly over top of pie, then pour raspberry sauce over entire top of pie, spreading evenly.

Refrigerate pie for 4 hours before serving—if you can wait that long—and enjoy!

View photos and tutorial of this recipe online at:

http://www.sexyveganmama.com/2011/07/deadline-schmedline-im-making-pie.html

Strawberry Lime Glacé Pie

If you love the Raspberry Lemonade Glacé Pie, you'll adore its sweet, tangy cousin, below.

Filling:

2 - 8 oz. tubs vegan cream cheese
1 c. cane juice crystals or natural sugar
1½ t. vanilla
¼ c. lime juice
2 T. cornstarch

Topping:

½ c. cane juice crystals or raw sugar
1 T. cornstarch
½ c. water
1 c. chopped fresh or frozen strawberries, thawed
½ c. sliced fresh or frozen strawberries, thawed

You'll also need:

One 9" unbaked pie crust, like Sexy Vegan Mama's Perfect Pie Crust, formed into a pie shell within a 9" pie pan.

Preheat oven to 350 degrees.

Combine filling ingredients in a blender or food processor.

Pour into unbaked pie crust and bake 45 to 50 minutes, or until top just begins to take on a golden hue, and the crust begins to brown.

Place baked pie on a cooling rack and allow to cool.

Prepare topping by combining cane juice crystals or sugar with cornstarch in a medium saucepan.

Gradually stir in water and chopped strawberries and cook over medium heat, stirring constantly, until mixture begins to thicken.

Bring to a boil and boil for 1 full minute while continuing to stir constantly to prevent burning.

Remove from heat.

Place sliced strawberries evenly over top of pie, and then pour strawberry sauce over entire top of pie, spreading evenly.

Refrigerate pie for 4 hours before serving.

Perfect Pumpkin Pie

Pumpkin pie is a holiday standard, and it's a shame for vegans to miss out on the spiced favorite. Try this recipe for your next family gathering—no one will suspect it's vegan!

1 t. lemon juice
1 c. vanilla soy milk
¼ c. unbleached flour
¼ c. oil
¾ c. cane juice crystals or natural sugar
¼ t. salt
1 – 15 oz. can pumpkin pie filling (not pureed pumpkin)
1 t. molasses

You'll also need:

One 9" unbaked pie crust, like Sexy Vegan Mama's Perfect Pie Crust, formed into a pie shell within a 9" pie pan.

Preheat oven 450 degrees.

In a small bowl, combine lemon juice and soy milk, and allow to curdle.

While waiting for the liquid to curdle, mix flour and oil into a paste.

Stir cane juice crystals or sugar and salt into flour mixture, blending thoroughly.

Add pumpkin pie filling and molasses to flour mixture, stirring until well combined.

Add curdled soy milk to pumpkin mixture and stir until smooth.

Pour into unbaked pie crust shell and bake for 15 minutes at 450 degrees, then turn oven down to 350 degrees and bake for 40 to 50 minutes longer. The pie filling may be bubbling, so be careful taking it out of the oven.

Let the pie cool thoroughly before serving. It's even better if you put it in the refrigerator to chill before serving.

Pumpkin Pecan Pie

Filling:

1 t. lemon juice
1 c. vanilla soy milk
¼ c. unbleached flour
¼ c. oil
¾ c. cane juice crystals or natural sugar
¼ t. salt
1 - 15 oz. can pumpkin pie filling (not pureed pumpkin)
1 t. molasses

Topping:

⅓ c. cane juice crystals or natural sugar
3 T. unbleached flour
3 T. cold vegan stick margarine
⅔ c. broken or coarsely chopped pecans

You'll also need:

One 9" unbaked pie crust, like Sexy Vegan Mama's Perfect Pie Crust, formed into a pie shell within a 9" pie pan.

Preheat oven 450 degrees.

In a small bowl, combine lemon juice and soy milk, and allow to curdle.

While waiting for the liquid to curdle, mix flour and oil into a paste.

Stir cane juice crystals or sugar and salt into flour mixture, blending thoroughly.

Add pumpkin pie filling and molasses to flour mixture, stirring until well combined.

Add curdled soy milk to pumpkin mixture and stir until smooth.

Pour into unbaked pie crust shell.

Combine cane juice crystals or sugar and flour for topping.

Cut in margarine, using a fork or pastry blender.

Stir in chopped pecans, and distribute pecan mixture evenly over top of filling.

Bake for 15 minutes at 450 degrees, then turn oven down to 350 degrees and bake for 40 to 50 minutes longer. The pie filling may be bubbling, so be careful taking it out of the oven.

Let the pie cool thoroughly before serving. It's even better if you put it in the refrigerator to chill before serving.

Deep-Dish French Apple Pie

As American as... Oh, well. The French topping on this pie is quick, simple, and delicious!

5 to 7 large (or 10 to 12 medium) Granny Smith apples, peeled and sliced (you'll need about 12 cups after slicing)
1½ c. cane juice crystals or natural sugar
½ c. unbleached flour
1 t. ground nutmeg
1 t. ground cinnamon

Topping:

1 c. unbleached flour
½ c. cane juice crystals or natural sugar
½ c. vegan stick margarine

You'll also need:

One 9" unbaked pie crust, like Sexy Vegan Mama's Perfect Pie Crust, formed into a pie shell within a 9" deep-dish pie pan.

Preheat oven to 425 degrees.

Combine cane juice crystals or sugar, flour, nutmeg and cinnamon, and then stir into apple slices.

Transfer sliced apples into unbaked pie crust shell (the apples should form a small mountain—they "cook down" a lot when baking).

Prepare topping by combining flour and sugar, then cutting in margarine until crumbly.

Spread topping evenly over apples in unbaked crust pie shell

Bake 35 minutes, then cover entire top with foil and bake another 10 to 15 minutes.

This pie is delicious served warm!

See photos and tutorial of this recipe online at:

http://www.sexyveganmama.com/2010/11/sexy-vegan-mama-deep-dish-french-apple.html

Coconut-Topped Fresh Pineapple Pie

Filling:

1 T. egg replacer powder, beaten with 4 T. water
¾ to 1 c. cane juice crystals or natural sugar (depending on sweetness of your pineapple)
3 T. unbleached flour
1½ T. lemon juice
4 c. diced fresh pineapple (about 1 medium pineapple)

You'll also need:

One 9" unbaked pie crust, like Sexy Vegan Mama's Perfect Pie Crust, formed into a pie shell within a 9" pie pan.

Coconut Topping:

½ T. egg replacer powder, beaten with 2 T. water
⅓ c. cane juice crystals or natural sugar
½ t. vanilla
2 T. soy milk
2¼ c. flaked coconut

Preheat oven to 375 degrees.

Filling Directions:

Beat egg replacer until frothy, and then mix in cane juice crystals or sugar, flour and lemon juice.

Fold in pineapple.

Fill unbaked crust pie shell with pineapple mixture.

Bake for 35 minutes.

While filling is baking, prepare topping.

Topping Directions:

Beat replacer egg with cane juice crystals or sugar until crystals dissolve.

Mix in vanilla and soy milk.

Fold in coconut until well-coated with "egg" mixture.

Remove pie from oven and cover evenly with coconut topping.

Return to oven for 20 minutes, or until crust and topping are brown.

Serve warm or at room temperature.

Pear Pasties

Christina-Marie's friend, Amy, from Montana, posted on a social media site a while ago about ordering pasties for a holiday party. To be perfectly honest, Christina-Marie, at the time, thought pasties were decorative sticky nipple covers—which led her to believe holidays were way more interesting in Montana.

As it turns out, pasties are, also, delicious little pockets full of yummy things. We don't recommend attaching these to your nipples.

This recipe is adapted from a standard that's been around for ages.

2 pears
¼ c. raisins
⅓ c. cane juice crystals or natural sugar
2 T. chopped nuts
1 T. "minute" tapioca
2 t. grated orange peel
Pastry for two-crust 9" pie, like Sexy Vegan Mama's Perfect Pie Crust

Orange Glaze:

¼ c. organic powdered sugar
Dash salt
¼ t. grated orange peel
1 T. orange juice

Preheat oven to 400 degrees.

Core and dice pears.

Combine pears, raisins, cane juice crystals or sugar, nuts, tapioca and orange peel.

Roll pastry ⅛" thick and cut into 4½" circles.

Divide pear mixture among pastry circles, depositing mixture in middle of each circle.

Fold pastry to form half-circles and seal edges with tines of fork; cut steam vent in each.

Bake for 25 to 30 minutes or until golden.

While pastries are baking, prepare Orange Glaze by combining powdered sugar, salt, orange peel and orange juice, blending well.

Drizzle with Orange Glaze while warm.

Grandma's Apple Crisp

Christina-Marie's mom isn't vegan, but everyone goes nuts over her apple crisp—her topping is light, sweet, and—appropriately—crispy. The following recipe is based upon that generations-old formula:

6 medium- to large-sized tart apples, like Granny Smith, Rome, or Pink Lady
1 T. lemon juice
½ c. cane juice crystals or natural sugar
3 T. unbleached flour
1½ t. cinnamon
½ t. nutmeg
⅔ c. unbleached flour
⅔ c. cane juice crystals or natural sugar
⅓ c. dairy-free stick margarine

Preheat oven to 350 degrees.

Peel, core and slice the apples into ¼" slices.

Put apple slices in a large bowl and sprinkle with lemon juice.

In a small bowl, mix together ½ cup cane juice crystals or sugar, flour, cinnamon, and nutmeg.

Toss sugar mixture together with sliced apples, stirring until apples are well-coated.

Place coated apples in a greased 9" square baking pan.

To make the topping, place flour, remaining cane juice crystals, or sugar and margarine in a medium bowl and blend with a pastry blender or fork tines until fine and crumbly.

Spread topping mix evenly on top of apples, and bake for 1 hour.

Serve while warm with vegan ice cream, or refrigerate for a delicious chilled dessert.

Grandma's Apple Brown Betty

Are you feeling your oats? This recipe is nearly identical to the apple crisp made by Christina-Marie's mother, except this one's Betty topping contains oats for a denser, chewier crust.

6 medium to large tart apples, like Granny Smith, Rome, or Pink Lady
1 T. lemon juice
½ c. cane juice crystals or natural sugar
3 T. unbleached flour
1½ t. cinnamon
½ t. nutmeg
½ c. unbleached flour
½ c. cane juice crystals or natural sugar
⅓ c. dairy-free stick margarine
½ c. oats

Preheat oven to 350 degrees.

Peel, core and slice the apples into ¼" slices.

Put apple slices in a large bowl and sprinkle with lemon juice.

In a small bowl, mix together ½ cup cane juice crystals or sugar, flour, cinnamon, and nutmeg.

Toss sugar mixture together with sliced apples, stirring until apples are well-coated.

Place coated apples in a greased 9" square baking pan.

To make the topping, place flour, remaining cane juice crystals, or sugar and margarine in a medium bowl and blend with a pastry blender or fork tines until fine and crumbly.

Stir in oats.

Spread topping mix evenly on top of apples, and bake for 1 hour.

Serve while warm with vegan ice cream, or refrigerate for a delicious chilled dessert.

BAKING WITH PHYLLO

Phyllo Basics

Christina-Marie used to be afraid of phyllo. She suspects it was because she grew up in her mom's bakery, and making baklava was An Event of Importance. Her mom couldn't make baklava unless someone else was working the counter, and there was nothing in the oven. She didn't take phone calls or respond to questions of a non-life-threatening variety.

Once she started working on baklava, a marching band could weave through the building and she wouldn't so much as look up.

So, just know that phyllo is scary to work with. If you become distracted while working with it, it'll dry out and shatter, and even your tears won't make it supple enough to form.

There are some tricks learned by the authors, though. Firstly, follow the thawing directions on the package precisely. Secondly, cover the stack of dough sheets with a layer of plastic wrap and cover the entire setup with a wet towel. Thirdly, make sure you don't have kids running around in the kitchen. (Wait until they're all asleep, or have some kind of magic nanny or a daycare person present.) Fourthly, put your phone away, and on a silent setting, nor set it down within your line of vision, either; you'll be tempted to respond to a text message or pick up the phone when your beloved other half calls...six times...without leaving a message.

In other words, prepare and focus.

After you've thawed and prepped your phyllo as directed on the package, each sheet of phyllo will be brushed with melted vegan margarine (some people use butter, but this is the authors' kitchens we're talking about, folks) before being shaped or formed.

Make sure your filling (whether it's vegetables, fruit, nuts or whatever), is ready to go, because you won't have time to throw it together once the margarine-brushing festivities begin.

When cutting phyllo, a long, sharp, non-serrated knife works best, used in a "pressing down" motion, rather than "sawing" it.

Raspberry "Cranes"

In Hiroshima, monuments and memorials are draped with strings of colorful paper cranes. They remind the authors of Sadako and the Thousand Paper Cranes, *and childhood experiments with origami paper. Fortunately, these pastries require slightly less patience and precision. They taste better, too.*

Please read Phyllo Basics before beginning. This recipe will make 6 "cranes."

1 c. frozen raspberries
½ c. cane juice crystals or natural sugar
2 T. cornstarch
¼ c. cold water
¼ to ½ c. dairy-free stick margarine, melted
6 phyllo sheets
6 t. vegan cream cheese (optional)

Use the back of a spoon to break raspberries into small chunks and put them in a medium saucepan.

Put cornstarch in a small bowl and gradually add water, stirring until smooth. Set aside.

Sprinkle cane juice crystals or sugar over raspberry chunks and heat over medium heat, stirring until crystals melt. The berries will begin to juice as the crystals dissolve, creating a berry syrup.

Gently increase heat to high. When syrup begins boiling, slowly pour in cornstarch mixture, stirring constantly.

Boil until filling thickens—about 1 or 2 minutes. Remove from heat and allow to cool. You may put it in the refrigerator, to speed cooling

Preheat oven to 325 degrees.

Slice a stack of 6 phyllo sheets, lengthwise, creating 12 long rectangles. Be sure to wrap up any remaining phyllo immediately and store according to package directions.

Lay one phyllo rectangle on your work surface, carefully covering remaining dough with plastic and a wet towel.

Brush with melted margarine. Place 1 to 2 Tablespoons raspberry filling, and an optional 1 teaspoon of cream cheese near the top left corner. Don't flatten the scoop of filling. You'll want a nice, compact ball to fold your pastry around.

Place another sheet of phyllo directly on top of the bottom sheet and filling, and brush with margarine.

Fold the top left corner down to meet the bottom edge of the rectangle, forming a folded-over triangle at the end, with the filling inside.

Fold the triangle over, then up, then over, and so on until you've formed a layered triangle, stuffed with filling.

Position your triangle so it looks like a mountain: longest side on the bottom with a peak at the top.

Fold the very tip of the peak over the bulge of filling, and then fold the remaining corners of the dough in and slightly up, crossing the "wings" of the pastry at the top.

Prop the folded pastry in a muffin tin cup, "wings" upward, folded sides facing outward so they have room to expand while baking.

Bake for 12 to 15 minutes, or until edges of pastry just begin to brown. Do not over bake. Allow to stand for 5 minutes before transferring to a cooling rack.

See photos and tutorial of this recipe online at:

http://www.sexyveganmama.com/2011/02/raspberry-cranes-fun-with-phyllo.html

Mini-Tart Phyllo Shells

Preformed phyllo mini-tart shells are available in the freezer section of many grocery stores, but they're a bit expensive, especially if you have a lot of mouths to feed. The authors make their own, using sheets of phyllo dough, and you can, too! Before you begin, please read Phyllo Basics for tips on handling the sheets of dough. This recipe makes 24 mini-tart shells.

12 sheets phyllo dough, thawed according to package directions
¼ to ½ cup vegan stick margarine

Preheat oven to 325 degrees.

Place 1 sheet on your work surface, taking care to recover remaining sheets.

Brush sheet with melted margarine, and then place another sheet of dough directly on top of the first.

Brush the second sheet with margarine and repeat until you have 6 stacked and "buttered" sheets of dough.

Using a long knife, cut the "buttered" dough into 24 equal sections. You should now have 24 thick "squares." (They may not be exactly square, but that's okay.)

Place a thick square in each of 24 mini-cupcake tin cups and push down into the cup. It won't cover the entire cup evenly, but that will be remedied with the next steps.

Repeat the process with the 6 remaining sheets of dough, but this time, push the squares into the cups on top of the first ones, staggering the corners so they are offset.

Turn all the corners down and in, making a "rim" around the top of the shell.

Bake for 12 to 14 minutes, or until the shells just begin to brown. They may be a little puffy when they come out of the oven. If so, while they're still hot, use the back of a spoon to gently push down the puffiness, opening up the shell's "cup" so it can be filled.

Fill with raspberry filling from Raspberry Cranes and top them with chocolate syrup, or use your favorite fruit filling.

If you're in a hurry, you can use canned pie filling or even jelly or jam.

See photos and tutorial of this recipe online at:

http://www.sexyveganmama.com/2011/02/mini-tart-shells-more-fun-with-phyllo.html

Egyptian Baklava

When Christina-Marie was an infant, her mother lived across the street from a friendly couple. One summer, the husband's mother came to visit from Egypt. She didn't speak English, and her daughter-in-law didn't speak Egyptian, so she was lonely for conversation. The Egyptian woman did, however, speak a little bit of French. Christina-Marie's mom had enough high school French under her belt to make small talk, and kept the visitor company while the woman's son was at work.

The woman asked Christina-Marie's mom to teach her how to make "American" bread, and, in return, she taught Christina-Marie's Mom how to make baklava. The recipe, below, was originally written in French by the woman for Christina-Marie's mother, and it has undergone very few alterations before inclusion here. Christina-Marie is honored in being able to pass it along.

1 lb. phyllo pastry sheets
3 sticks vegan margarine
2 c. chopped almonds or walnuts
¼ c. cane juice crystals or natural sugar
2 tsp. ground cinnamon
2 c. cane juice crystals or natural sugar
1 c. water
4 tsp. lemon juice
1 tsp. vanilla extract
Whole cloves (optional)

Place nuts, ¼ cup cane juice crystals, or sugar and cinnamon in blender or food processor. Pulse until nuts are finely chopped and sugar and cinnamon are well blended.

Melt margarine and clarify by skimming water off top of melted margarine. Using a pastry brush and part of the melted butter, grease a large cookie sheet with sides.

Place 1 phyllo sheet in the greased cookie sheet, brushing sheet with melted margarine.

Place another sheet on top of the first and brush with melted margarine.

Continue to layer phyllo sheets, brushing each with melted margarine, until you have 4 or 5 sheets.

Sprinkle approximately ½ cup cinnamon-nut mixture

evenly over the stack of phyllo sheets.

Repeat again: 4 or 5 phyllo sheets—each brushed with melted margarine—then sprinkle with ½ cup cinnamon-nut mixture. Continue to repeat until you have used all of the phyllo and nut mixture.

End the layering process with phyllo sheets and melted margarine.

Cut pastry into desired size, in triangle or diamond shapes.

Bake at 350 degrees for 30 minutes or until golden brown. While pastry is baking, prepare the syrup.

Combine remaining cane juice crystals or sugar, water and lemon juice in small saucepan. Bring to a boil and boil gently for 8 minutes.

Remove from heat and add vanilla extract. Set aside until pastry is baked.

Pour syrup over baked pastry while it is still hot.

Let set for at least 1 hour (overnight is even better if you can wait that long).

DOUGHNUTS AND OTHER DEEP-FRIED SINS

Whole Wheat Churros

These fried dough pastries are traditionally rolled in cinnamon and sugar after being pushed through a tube with a star-shaped tip. Now, we're all for tradition, but using a whole wheat flour—thicker and heavier than white flour—makes it difficult to press through a decorating-bag tip, and not everyone has a specialty bakery press in their kitchen. Reusable pastry bags, without a tip, work just fine. If you don't have a decorating bag, you can use a heavy-duty plastic bag (like a name-brand freezer bag), with the corner cut off.

In any event, these are delicious, even with their smooth edges.

1 c. water
2 T. cane juice crystals or natural sugar
½ t. salt
1 T. oil
1 c. whole wheat flour
Oil for frying

⅓ c. cane juice crystals or natural sugar
1 t. cinnamon

You'll also need:

A candy thermometer to check oil temperature

In a saucepan, stir together water, 2 Tablespoons of cane juice crystals or sugar, salt, and Tablespoon of oil. Bring to a gentle boil, and remove from heat.

Stir in flour to make a dough.

In a deep wok, frying pan or deep-fryer, heat frying oil to 350 degrees.

Load dough into a decorating bag (or heavy-duty plastic bag with the corner cut off) and squeeze out finger-sized strips of dough into oil.

Fry the strips for 60 to 90 seconds, or until the outsides are a deep, golden brown. Use tongs or a slotted spoon to remove from oil, and drain on paper towels.

Stir together remaining cane juice crystals or sugar and cinnamon, then roll drained pastries in sugar mixture.

Serve warm.

See photos and tutorial of this recipe online at:

http://www.sexyveganmama.com/2011/08/recipe-whole wheat-churros.html

Jelly-Filled Sugar Doughnuts

These little pockets of sweetness are perhaps the very reason to have a fryer. Don't have one yourself? That's okay! You can use a deep wok to fry these babies up! Makes 24 doughnuts.

1 c. warm water (you're looking for "baby-bath water" warm—too hot, and you'll kill your yeast)
1½ T. yeast
⅓ c. cane juice crystals or natural sugar
1 c. vanilla soy milk
2 T. oil
½ t. vanilla
4 c. unbleached flour
½ t. salt
Additional flour for rolling
Vegan jelly or jam for filing (we used strawberry)
Additional cane juice crystals or natural sugar for dusting
Several cups oil for frying

You'll also need:

A candy thermometer to check oil temperature

In a medium bowl, sprinkle yeast over warm water and allow to dissolve.

Add cane juice crystals or sugar, soy milk, oil, and vanilla. Stir until cane juice or sugar crystals dissolve.

In a large bowl, combine flour and salt.

Gradually add liquid mixture to flour and salt, stirring until all liquid is incorporated, and a stiff dough forms.

Cover bowl with a damp towel and allow to rise for 1 hour.

Dump dough onto a floured surface and knead for 1 to 2 minutes, then roll out into a large rectangle, about ½" thick.

Cut rectangle into 24 squares and place 1 teaspoon of vegan jelly in the middle.

Gather the corners of each square to form a ball, with the jelly sealed inside.

Gently flatten the balls back to about ¾". Don't worry—they'll puff back up during the frying process.

Allow doughnuts to rise for an additional 30 minutes, or until doubled in size.

In a deep fryer or wok, heat enough oil to cover the doughnuts to 350 degrees. Use a candy thermometer to check the oil temperature.

Fry doughnuts for 1 to 2 minutes on each side to

achieve a golden brown finish.

Remove from oil and drain on paper towels until cool enough to handle, and then dust each in cane juice crystals or sugar. Tip: Pour sugar into a large bowl, drop doughnuts in, and then flip over for a nice, even coating.

See photos and tutorial of this recipe online at:

http://www.sexyveganmama.com/2011/10/vegan-jelly-filled-sugar-donuts-happy.html

Peanut Butter Banana Old-Fashioned Doughnuts

Elvis Presley is rumored to have loved deep-fried peanut butter banana sandwiches. In a tribute to The King, we offer you something even tastier—Peanut Butter Banana Old-Fashioned Doughnuts! This recipe has been adapted from one found online for Samoan Panikekes—crispy, fried banana pancakes—but after all the meddling, we've been left with an awesome doughnut with a crisp shell and soft inside that reminds Christina-Marie of the old-fashioned doughnuts her mom made in her bakery, years ago. These are very rich, and delicious with coffee.

3½ c. unbleached flour
1½ c. cane juice crystals or natural sugar
1 T. baking powder
2 bananas, pureed

⅓ c. creamy peanut butter
½ T. vanilla extract
1½ c. soy milk or other non-dairy milk

You'll also need:

Several cups oil for frying
Candy thermometer to check oil temperature
Fryer or deep wok to fry in
Small scoop or two large spoons

In a large bowl, combine flour, cane juice crystals or sugar and baking powder.

Add pureed bananas, peanut butter, vanilla extract, and soy milk, blending well.

Heat oil to 350 degrees.

Using a scoop, drop about 1 Tablespoon and a half of dough into oil and fry about 3 minutes or until doughnuts float to top of oil and have a crisp brown crust.

If using spoons, scoop dough up with one spoon, and then use another to push the ball of dough off into the oil.

Remove from oil and drain on paper towels.

See photos of this recipe online at:

http://www.sexyveganmama.com/2011/10/doughnut-be-cruel-peanut-butter-banana.html

"Bacon" Maple Bars

Vegan bacon substitutes are commercially available, but they tend to be a bit pricey. In the quest for a passable vegan bacon maple bar, we decided to make our own—for much less money. Any of those commercial "fakin' bacon" products will work just fine atop this doughnut, should you choose not to make our cheapo version.

Bacon maple-bar lovers describe this treat as breakfast in a bar, combining the flavors of pancakes, syrup and bacon. Why should vegans be left out of the craze popping up in bakeries across the nation? It's time they had our own "breakfast in a bar!" This recipe makes 18 to 24 maple bars.

"Bacon" Ingredients:

1 lb. firm or extra-firm tofu (not silken), drained
¼ c. soy sauce, shoyu, tamari or liquid aminos
¼ c. apple cider vinegar
¼ c. water
2 T. cane juice crystals or natural sugar
½ t. onion powder
½ t. garlic powder
½ t. ground ginger
½ t. maple flavoring
Oil for frying

Doughnut Ingredients:

½ c. warm water ("baby bath water" warm, or you'll kill your yeast)
2 T. active yeast
1 c. soy milk
¼ c. plus 2 T. vegan stick margarine
1 t. salt
½ c. cane juice crystals or natural sugar
1 c. cold water
1½ T. egg replacer powder, prepared with 6 T. warm water
5 to 7 c. unbleached flour
Oil for frying

You'll also need:

Candy thermometer to check oil temperature

Frosting Ingredients:

5 c. organic powdered sugar
½ c. vegan stick margarine
¼ c. soy milk
2 T. maple flavoring

"Bacon" Directions, Part One:

Slice drained tofu into ⅛ to ¼" slices, and then cut slices in half to create strips.

Arrange strips in a 9" x 13" baking dish (it's okay if

they overlap a bit).

Put remaining ingredients into a blender and mix until cane juice crystals or sugar dissolve. The liquid will be frothy.

Pour liquid over tofu strips and allow to marinate while you prepare your doughnuts.

Doughnut Directions:

Pour ½ cup water into a large bowl and sprinkle yeast over top to dissolve. Set aside.

In a saucepan, scald the soy milk.

Add margarine, salt and cane juice crystals or sugar to scalded soy milk and stir until cane juice crystals are dissolved.

Add cold water and prepared egg replacer to soy milk mixture and stir well.

Allow soy milk mixture to cool to "baby bath water" warm, then pour into large bowl with dissolved yeast and stir well.

Add flour to liquid, stirring in 1 cup at a time, until a soft, elastic dough forms. Add more flour as necessary to make the dough workable and prevent sticking to hands or bowl.

Flour a large working surface and turn the dough out, rolling into a large rectangle, about ¼" thick.

Cut dough into 18 to 24 bars; about 3" x 6".

Space the bars 1" to 2" apart, and let rise until doubled—about 1 hour.

Heat enough oil to cover doughnuts in a deep frying pan, wok or fryer to 350 degrees.

Carefully drop bars into hot oil and fry until golden brown—about 1 minute on each side.

Remove from oil and drain on paper towels.

Allow to cool before frosting.

Frosting Directions:

In a stand mixer or by hand, combine all ingredients and blend until smooth.

Add more powdered sugar or soy milk to achieve desired consistency.

"Bacon" Directions, Part Two:

In a deep frying pan, wok or fryer, heat enough oil to cover tofu strips to 375 to 400 degrees.

Carefully (oil may "pop!") place strips in hot oil and

fry until crispy, then remove from oil and drain on paper towels.

Assembly:

Frost cooled doughnut bars with maple frosting, then top each maple bar with 1 strip of "bacon."

See photos and tutorial of this recipe online at:

http://www.sexyveganmama.com/2012/01/vegan-bacon-maple-bars.html

Better Than NOLA Beignets

In New Orleans, a short walk from Bourbon Street, is a café which has become quite famous for its beignets. Many a (very) late night, Christina-Marie stumbled with friends into the eatery and ordered "just black coffee, thanks" while her cohorts indulged in powdered-sugar dusted, deep-fried delicacies. Enough of that, thank you very much. It's time for a brilliant beignet, of a better batter. Let the Age of the Vegan Beignet begin!

1½ c. warm water ("baby bath water" warm)
1½ T. dry active yeast
1¾ c. unbleached flour
¾ t. salt
2 T. cane juice crystals or natural sugar
½ t. vanilla

½ t. lemon juice
Several cups oil for frying
Organic powdered sugar for garnish
Dairy-free chocolate syrup for garnish (optional)

You'll also need:

Candy thermometer to check oil temperature

In a medium bowl, sprinkle yeast over water and allow to dissolve.

In a large bowl, combine flour, salt and cane juice crystals or sugar.

Add vanilla and lemon juice to yeast mixture and stir until well-mixed.

Pour wet ingredients into dry, stirring to create a soft dough.

Cover bowl with a damp towel and allow to rise for 45 minutes. The batter should be airy and light when done rising.

Heat oil in a fryer, wok or deep pan to 350 degrees.

Drop large spoonfuls of batter into hot oil, taking care not to crowd the beignets as they fry. Cook for 1 to 2 minutes on each side, or until golden brown.

Remove from oil, drain on paper towels, and serve

with a dusting of powdered sugar and—if desired—chocolate syrup.

See photos and tutorial of this recipe online at:

http://www.sexyveganmama.com/2012/05/better-than-nola-vegan-beignets.html

FROZEN FANCIES

Tropical Fruit Sorbet

This simple sorbet is delicious when prepared with guava or pineapple juice. It can be scooped and floated in a punchbowl filled with lemon-lime soda for a party, served in a cone, or enjoyed in a chilled glass midsummer by the pool. Poolside is our preferred way to go, of course!

1 ripe mango or papaya
½ c. water or fruit juice of your choice
¼ c. cane juice crystals or natural sugar
2 T. fresh lemon juice

Remove peel and seeds from fruit, then puree in blender or food processor.

Heat water or fruit juice and cane juice crystals or sugar to boiling.

Boil 1 minute, or until crystals are dissolved.

Add lemon juice and stir.

Cool slightly and mix with fruit puree.

Place mixture into ice cube trays and freeze at least 4 hours or overnight.

Put frozen fruit cubes into food processor or blender, and process until mixture is smooth and soft, then transfer to serving bowl and return to freezer for 30 minutes or longer, or until ready to serve.

Cranberry Orange Sorbet

Christina-Marie asked her teen daughters, "Pepper" and "GirlWonder," to test-drive this recipe for the cookbook. The results tasted fantastic, but the girls' very literal reading of the recipe led them to stuff all the cranberries and syrup into the blender at once, causing a cranberry explosion throughout the kitchen. Our advice? Be ye not so literal, and divide the cooked cranberries into two batches, if necessary. Unless, of course, you want to end up, like Christina-Marie, scrubbing berry syrup off cabinets, floor... and ceiling.

For 1 quart sorbet you will need:

3 c. frozen cranberries
1½ c. water
3½ c. cane juice crystals or natural sugar
½ c. orange juice
¼ c fresh lemon juice
1 T. grated orange rind

Grated orange rind or mint sprigs for garnish

Put cranberries in medium saucepan with water and cane juice crystals or sugar.

Heat to boiling and simmer gently, stirring occasionally, for 10 minutes.

Transfer to blender or food processor and blend until smooth. Add orange juice, lemon juice and orange rind.

Turn into shallow pan and freeze 4 to 6 hours, or until solid.

Break up sorbet and place into food processor or blender. Process until light and fluffy.

Store fluffed sorbet in covered container in freezer. When serving, garnish with grated orange rind or mint sprigs, if desired.

See photos of this recipe online at:

http://www.sexyveganmama.com/2012/05/cranberry-orange-sorbet.html

Pineapple Creamsicle Vegan Sherbet

This recipe is a sweet, cholesterol-free twist on the dye-filled orange sherbet which graces the tables of elementary school cafeterias. Even better, it can be enjoyed at home by big kids and little kids alike—

without that peculiar cafeteria smell.

½ c. vanilla soy milk
½ c. cane juice crystals or natural sugar
4 T. instant pectin granules (look for these in the canning section of your supermarket)
1 - 20 oz. can of pineapple, in its own juice, juice included
Juice of 3 oranges
1 T. lemon juice

In a saucepan, combine soy milk, cane juice crystals or sugar and pectin, stirring over medium heat until sugar is dissolved. Remove from heat.

In a blender or food processor, blend pineapple and its juice until smooth.

Add juice from oranges and lemon juice, blending until well-combined.

Stir blended fruit and juice mixture into soy milk mixture, mixing thoroughly.

Pour sherbet into the bottom of a 9" x 13" baking dish (the shallow depth of the sherbet will help it freeze more quickly) and freeze for 1 to 2 hours, or until "scoopable."

Tip: For extra-smooth, extra-creamy sherbet, blend the mixture a second time after the first freeze, then return to freezer until firm.

Scoop, and serve in a chilled glass.

See photos of this recipe online at:

http://www.sexyveganmama.com/2011/08/recipe-pineapple-creamsicle-vegan.html

Berry Mango Vegan Frozen Yogurt

Frozen yogurt shops are popping up all over, offering all manner of creamy treats. We see no reason for those watching their cholesterol or following a vegan diet to miss out on the craze. Try this delicious "froyo," scooped into a sugar cone or served in a chilled dish.

1 c. vanilla soy yogurt
½ c. frozen raspberries or blackberries
Meat of 1 mango, diced
¼ c. cane juice crystals or natural sugar
2 T. instant pectin (find this in your supermarket, with the canning supplies)

Blend all ingredients in a blender or food processor until smooth.

Pour into the bottom of a 9" x 13" baking dish. The shallow depth of the yogurt mixture helps it freeze more quickly.

Freeze for 1½ to 2 hours, or until scoopable.

Mango Pomegranate Coconut Ice Cream

Choosing a vegan diet shouldn't mean the end of ice cream. This recipe is adapted from one found on the RAWk Me! blog at http://rawgirlinmumbai.blogspot.com, and is loaded with fruity flavor and rich, creamy coconut milk.

1 pomegranate
1 mango
½ c. cane juice crystals or natural sugar
1 13.5 oz. can coconut milk, full fat
½ t. vanilla

Peel pomegranate. Remove pulp and seeds and puree in a blender. Set puree aside.

Peel mango and cut the fruit away from pit. Puree mango in blender and add pureed pomegranate.

Add vanilla, cane juice crystals or sugar and half the can of coconut milk to the blender pitcher and blend well.

When crystals are dissolved, add the rest of the coconut milk and blend until everything is well-mixed and frothy.

Transfer mixture to a deep-dish pie pan or deep cake pan and freeze for 1 hour. At this point, ice cream will harden a bit on top but still be creamy beneath the surface.

Scoop out ice cream and return to blender. Blend until smooth and put back into pan and freeze for 3 to 4 hours.

Serve in a chilled dish, and garnish with a sprig of mint and a mango slice, if desired.

See photos and tutorial of this recipe online at:

http://www.sexyveganmama.com/2011/01/recipe-mango-pomegranate-coconut-ice.html

Tropical Schnappsicles

This recipe is for the daiquiri-loving, "cool" grown-ups hanging out by the pool, craving a tasty treat with a little kick. You can substitute your favorite liqueur, vodka, tequila or rum for the peach schnapps in this recipe.

Meat of 2 mangoes, chopped
1 c. fresh or frozen raspberries
1½ oz. peach schnapps or other liqueur of choice
2 T. cane juice crystals or natural sugar
Juice of one lime
½ c. pineapple juice
Handful fresh mint leaves (preferably grabbed
    directly from your garden)

In a blender, puree mangoes and raspberries.

Add schnapps, cane juice crystals or natural sugar, and fruit juices, blending until smooth. Add mint leaves and pulse until leaves are chopped into tiny flecks.

Pour into ice pop molds and freeze.

Tip: If the pops are difficult to remove from molds after freezing, run them under a little hot water, until the pops slide out easily.

See photos and tutorial of this recipe online at:

http://www.sexyveganmama.com/2011/08/tropical-schnappsicles-grown-up-ice.html

Carrot "Yogurt" Pops

Christina-Marie shamelessly tricked a young child into eating fruits and vegetables by blending them into this dessert. Considering how delicious these pops are, Christina-Marie remains guilt-free and stands by her sneak attack.

3 carrots
2 apples
1 banana
1 c. vegan vanilla soy yogurt

You'll also need:

A juicer

Juice carrots and apples.

In a blender, puree banana until smooth.

Add yogurt and carrot-apple juice to blender pitcher and blend all until well-mixed.

Pour into ice pop molds and freeze.

Tip: If frozen pops are difficult to remove from molds, run some hot water over the outside of the molds, until the pops slide out easily.

See photos of this recipe online at:

http://www.sexyveganmama.com/2011/08/want-your-kids-to-eat-their-veggies.html

CANDIES AND MUNCHIES

Macadamia Coconut Toffee

Christina-Marie's husband says this toffee is "too good for the kids and should be saved only for company." Except... it never lasts until company arrives. Christina-Marie blames Mr. Wright, but he says there must be a scientific phenomenon going on, similar to evaporation. Now, science isn't Christina-Marie's or my forte, but there is something decidedly suspicious, at such times, about her husband's toffee breath.

1 c. vegan stick margarine
1 c. cane juice crystals or natural sugar
3 T. water
1 T. light corn syrup
⅔ c chopped macadamia nuts
8 oz. dairy-free chocolate chips
⅓ c. flaked coconut

You'll also need:

Candy thermometer to check temperature

Melt margarine in heavy 2 quart saucepan over low heat.

Add cane juice crystals or sugar and stir, until mixture starts to boil.

Combine water and corn syrup; blend into sugar mixture.

Cook and stir over medium heat until mixture comes to a boil. Reduce heat, cover and cook 3 minutes.

Uncover and cook gently, stirring frequently to prevent burning, until a small amount of mixture forms a hard and brittle thread in cold water (or to a temperature of 300 degrees).

Remove from heat.

Stir in ⅓ cup macadamia nuts, and spread toffee evenly in well-buttered 9" x 13" baking dish. Let stand until almost cool to the touch.

Melt ½ of the chocolate in saucepan over very low heat, stirring constantly until smooth. Spread over toffee, and then sprinkle with ⅓ cup macadamia nuts.

Let stand until chocolate is firm.

Turn toffee out onto waxed paper.

Melt remaining ½ of chocolate and spread over bottom

of toffee, then sprinkle with flaked coconut. Let stand until chocolate is firm, then break into pieces.

Makes about 1.5 pounds of toffee.

See photos of this recipe online at:

http://www.sexyveganmama.com/2012/05/macadamia-coconut-toffee.html

Peanut Chews

9 c. corn flakes
1½ c. cane juice crystals or natural sugar
¼ t. salt
¾ c. light corn syrup
¼ c. vegan stick margarine
¾ c. water
2 t. vanilla
½ c. crunchy peanut butter

You'll also need:

Candy thermometer to check temperature

Place corn flakes in a very large bowl.

In a large saucepan, combine cane juice crystals or sugar, salt, corn syrup, margarine and water.

Bring to a boil and reduce heat.

Cook to hard ball stage (250 degrees), using care not to overcook.

Remove from heat and stir in vanilla and peanut butter.

Pour over corn flakes, tossing with a large spoon to completely cover flakes with syrup.

IMPORTANT: WORK QUICKLY.

Drop mixture in 2" to 3" clusters onto waxed paper. Makes about 40 clusters.

Sexy Vegan Mama's Rum (or Liqueur) Balls

Says Christina-Marie: "This recipe, my friends, is the one which started the glorious collaboration between Wright and Maltese. We were both to read at an event, which promised not only our stellar wit and dramatics, but also cookies.

"Now, cookies are all well and good, but I find if I'm desperate for a good turnout, the promise of booze is much more effective than my sparkling personality. After all, I don't have the credentials of Mr. Maltese. That's why I made rum balls. Well, not just rum balls, but also Southern Comfort® balls and Kahlua® balls.

A meeting of the minds (and stomachs) was created, and the spark of collaboration began."

You, too, can bribe your loved ones with these grown-up treats. Here's how:

- ½ - 14.4-oz. box of vegan graham crackers (check for honey and dairy)
- 1¼ c. organic powdered sugar
- 3 T. unsweetened cocoa powder
- 1 c. slivered almonds
- ½ c. rum, liqueur or flavored alcohol of your choice *(vanilla vodka, peppermint schnapps, brandy, Gran Marnier®, butterscotch schnapps...)*
- 3 T. light corn syrup
- ¾ c. cocoa powder, organic powdered sugar, cane juice crystals or natural sugar for rolling

Whiz the graham crackers in a blender or food processor until they are very finely ground and almost powdery.

Very finely chop the almonds with a knife or in a blender or food processor until they are in small, coarse bits.

Mix all the dry ingredients—except the cocoa or sugar you've set aside for rolling—in a large bowl.

Add liqueur and corn syrup and stir until well mixed. Your arm will get very tired, and you may need to use more liquor (if your dough is too dry, you can put some more in the mixture, as well as in your belly). The dough should be stiff and sticky, and hold its shape when rolled into a ball.

Form into 1" balls (a melon baller works well), rolling with the palms of your clean hands.

Roll each ball in the cocoa, powdered sugar, or natural sugar, coating well.

Line the bottom of a covered container with wax paper and place the balls inside, in a single layer.

Put the container in the refrigerator for 2 to 3 days before serving, and threaten bodily harm to anyone who tries to sneak any before they're cured.

See photos of this recipe online at:

http://www.sexyveganmama.com/2010/12/let-get-ready-to-rum-ball-recipe-sexy.html

Cream Cheese Mints

After years of passing up creamy mints (hello, dairy and gelatin) at every wedding, restaurant and social function, Christina-Marie was thrilled to find a recipe for cream cheese mints in her mother's recipe box. With a bit of tweaking, she created this vegan version. Can you stand the "excite-mint?" This recipe makes four dozen sweet mints.

4 oz. vegan cream cheese
⅛ c. vegan stick margarine
1 to 1½ lb. organic powdered sugar
few drops food coloring: red, yellow, green, or as desired
¼ t. peppermint, wintergreen or lemon extract

Combine cream cheese and margarine in heavy-bottomed saucepan.

Stir over low heat until cream cheese is soft, margarine is melted, and mixture is thoroughly blended.

Add the powdered sugar and stir until well combined, forming a thick dough which holds its shape when rolled.

Add your choice of food coloring and flavoring. If desired, you may divide the batch to make multiple color choices or flavors.

Roll into 1" balls. Place on a sheet of wax paper.

Press with a fork, or stamp with decorative cookie stamp to form a design on top.

Let stand, uncovered, about 4 hours or overnight, until mints are firm and outside is dry, but inside is still moist and creamy.

See photos and tutorial of this recipe online at:

http://www.sexyveganmama.com/2012/05/vegan-cream-cheese-mints.html

Chocolate Marzipan Roll

Marzipan is one of those sweets often made into art, molded into whimsical shapes to be enjoyed separately, or as cake adornments. This less labor-intensive recipe creates a marzipan roll, which is simply beautiful as embellished with a few almonds. Of course, if you're crafty, you may use the recipe as a base for your next sculpting project. Go ahead, knock yourself out.

1 - 8 oz. can almond paste
2 T. light corn syrup
1¾ c. organic powdered sugar
2 T. cocoa
1 T. vegan margarine
2 t. coffee- or chocolate-flavored liqueur or vanilla extract
½ c. dairy-free chocolate chips
1 T. vegan stick margarine
15 whole blanched almonds

Cut almonds paste into small pieces and put into bowl.

Add corn syrup and 1 cup of the powdered sugar. Knead until smooth.

Roll out ¾ of the mixture between 2 sheets of wax paper into a 10-inch square.

Add remaining powdered sugar, cocoa, margarine and liqueur to remaining almond paste mixture. Knead until well blended. Mixture will be stiff.

Shape into a ball. Place between sheets of wax paper and roll out into a 10-inch square.

Remove wax paper from first square. Place on top of chocolate-flavored square. For a light-colored roll, place chocolate square on top of first square.

Roll up tightly, using wax paper to assist in rolling.

Wrap roll in plastic wrap and chill for 1 to 2 hours.

Melt margarine and chocolate chips on stovetop over lowest heat.

Remove roll from refrigerator and discard plastic wrap. Frost top of roll with melted chocolate.

Decorate with almonds, making 3 five-petal flowers on top of roll. Return to refrigerator to chill until ready to serve, and then slice into rounds.

See photos and tutorial of this recipe online at:

http://www.sexyveganmama.com/2012/05/vegan-chocolate-marzipan-roll.html

Almond and Sour Cream Candy

Have you ever made—say, a batch of fudge, brownies, cookies or candy—and accidentally eaten the entire thing yourself? We're not saying Christina-Marie once ate all 36 squares of delicious candy resulting from this recipe, but... We're not saying she didn't, either.

2 c. cane juice crystals or natural sugar
⅛ t. salt
1 c. vegan sour cream
⅛ t. ground cinnamon
½ t. vanilla
3 drops almond extract
1 c. slivered almonds

You'll also need:

Candy thermometer to check temperature

Mix cane juice crystals or sugar, salt and sour cream in a heavy two-quart saucepan.

Heat gently over low heat, without stirring, to soft ball stage (245 degrees). Remove from heat.

Cool to lukewarm (110 degrees), then add cinnamon and flavorings and beat until creamy.

Fold in almonds. Pour into greased 8" square pan. When cool, cut into squares.

Makes 36 squares.

See photos and tutorial of this recipe online at:

http://www.sexyveganmama.com/2012/05/vegan-almond-and-sour-cream-candy.html

Macadamia Almond Microwave Brittle

1 c. cane juice crystals or natural sugar
½ c. light corn syrup
¾ c. coarsely chopped macadamia nuts
¾ c. coarsely chopped almonds
1 T. vegan stick margarine
2 t. vanilla extract
1 t. baking soda

Combine cane juice crystals or sugar and corn syrup in a two-quart microwave-safe bowl.

Microwave on high for 5 minutes.

Stir in nuts.

Microwave on high for 4 to 5 minutes, or until a candy thermometer reads 300 degrees (hard-crack stage).

Quickly stir in margarine; vanilla and baking soda until mixture is light and foamy.

When bubbles subside, pour onto a greased cookie sheet, spreading as thinly as possible with a metal spatula.

Cool completely and break into pieces.

Store in an airtight container with wax paper between layers.

Makes about 1 pound of brittle.

Easy-Peasy Peanut Brittle

2 c. cane juice crystals or natural sugar
1 T. vegan stick margarine
½ t. baking soda
1 c. peanuts
⅛ t. salt

In a heavy-bottomed saucepan over medium heat, stir together cane juice crystals or sugar and margarine until smooth, and crystals dissolve.

Remove immediately from heat.

Add salt, peanuts, and baking soda.

Stir only until blended.

Pour quickly onto well-buttered sheet. Cool completely, and then break into pieces.

Store in an airtight container.

Quick Peanut Popcorn Balls

Great for the kids! Or, make mini-sized versions, and pile them on a platter for a party. Or, sneak them into the movie theater. If you get caught, we never spoke, okay?

½ c. light corn syrup
¼ c. cane juice crystals or natural sugar
¾ c. creamy or chunky peanut butter
8 c. plain popped corn

In a one-quart saucepan, mix corn syrup and cane juice crystals or sugar.

Cook over medium heat, stirring constantly, until mixture comes to boil and crystals dissolve.

Remove from heat and stir in peanut butter until smooth.

Immediately pour mixture over popped corn in large bowl. Stir until evenly coated.

Grease or "butter" hands and shape into eight 2½" balls.

Frankie's Fab Caramel Corn

Christina-Marie's friend, Frankie, provided the original, non-vegan, version of this recipe and is owed some sort of Cosa Nostra favor for having shared it, according to her accompanying, "Someday—and that day may never come—I'll call upon you to do a service for me. But until that day..."

1 c. unpopped popcorn, popped in air popper, divided into two 9" x 13" baking dishes
1¼ c. cane juice crystals or natural sugar
½ c. vegan stick margarine
1 t. vanilla extract
1 T. water
pinch of salt
1 t. baking soda

Preheat oven to 200 degrees.

Over medium heat, melt together cane juice crystals or sugar, margarine, vanilla extract, water and salt.

Bring to boil, and continue to boil for 5 minutes.

Remove from heat and add baking soda, stirring quickly.

Pour over popcorn and mix. Work quickly, as the caramel begins to harden as soon as it starts cooling.

Bake for 1 hour, stirring every 15 minutes.

WILLIAM Comments on Xocai® Healthy Chocolate®

Xocai® Healthy Chocolate® is pure, unprocessed cacao that is blanched, unfermented, sun-dried, non-roasted, non-alkalized, non lechinized, and, via a patented coldpress process, retains the maximum amount of antioxidants in the finished product, making it far healthier than commercially heat-processed chocolate ("candy").

This book's following two recipes are the results of my conversion to the belief that Xocai® Healthy Chocolate® products are truly beneficial to good health, my having become an Independent Distributor, and my determination to promote them by including, whenever possible, at least one original recipe including Xocai® Healthy Chocolate® in any cookbook I write on my own or in collaboration with others.

While not all of the Xocai® Healthy Chocolate® products are "right" for the vegan life-style, there is at least one of them, Xocai® Nuggets, that fit the bill, and those are the ones Christina-Marie and I have included as ingredients here.

For more on Xocai® Healthy Chocolate®, feel free to contact me via:

http://www.mxi.myvoffice.com/williammaltese

Xocai®: Trifling with Truffles

For the most intense sweet tooth, we prescribe these creamy truffles—made with healthy Xocai® chocolate, to reduce the potential for guilt. We don't do guilt, and we don't even attempt to play psychologist. Can you imagine? "I hear you saying you have unresolved issues with your childhood, which are holding you back in your current relationships, and impeding your progress toward self-actualization. Okay. Take two Xocai® truffles, and call someone else."

When working with Xocai®, it's important to know it's a cold-processed product, and most of the healthy benefits of the chocolate are essentially destroyed at temperatures over 100 degrees. You'll need a candy thermometer to check the temperature of the chocolate as it melts.

8 oz. vegan cream cheese
Approximately 6 c. organic powdered sugar
½ T. vanilla extract
⅛ to ¼ c. finely chopped Xocai® Nuggets
Cocoa powder, shredded coconut, finely chopped nuts
    OR 1 finely grated Xocai® Nugget for rolling

Place cream cheese in blender or food processor and blend until creamy.

Add ⅓ of powdered sugar to blender and process until well-mixed. Add second ⅓ and process again until thoroughly mixed.

Add vanilla and blend. Transfer cream cheese mixture to a bowl. DO NOT CHILL.

To melt the chopped Xocai® Nuggets, place chocolate in a small bowl, then place small bowl into a medium bowl.

Carefully fill medium bowl around small bowl with warm water, no hotter than 100 degrees. Using this "double-boiler" method protects the chocolate from high heat.

Stir chopped Xocai® Nuggets as they begin to melt to distribute warmth. If water begins to cool, add some hot water to the outer bowl, ensuring the combined temperature of the water does not reach over 100 degrees.

While chocolate is melting, add remaining ⅓ of powdered sugar to cream cheese mixture and use clean hands to work the powdered sugar in. The warmth from your hands will take the chill from the cream cheese mixture, ensuring the warmed chocolate will not clump when it is added.

Add melted chocolate to cream cheese mixture, again mixing with hands, until well-mixed. Cover bowl and chill for 1 hour.

Shape chilled dough into 1" balls, and then roll in garnish of choice. Store left over truffles in a sealed container in the refrigerator or freezer.

View photos and tutorial of this recipe online at:

http://www.sexyveganmama.com/2012/05/xocai-trifling-with-truffles.html

Xocai® Peanut Butter Fudge

As discussed in our preceding recipe for Xocai® Trifling with Truffles, it is important to watch the temperature when melting the chocolate, in order to prevent loss of those awesome health benefits. If we're going to eat chocolate—and that's likely a given—we want it to kick our bodies into gear in order to be well-rested to eat the next batch of chocolate.

Also, there's a fair amount of stirring involved in this recipe. Your arm may get tired. Have some Xocai® first, for a burst of energy. We're just sayin'.

½ c. vegan stick margarine, plus a bit more to "butter" the pan
1 c. creamy or chunky peanut butter
1 c. cane juice crystals or natural sugar
8 oz. vegan cream cheese
¼ to ½ c. finely chopped Xocai® Nuggets

In a heavy-bottomed saucepan, heat margarine, peanut butter, cane juice crystals or sugar, and cream cheese, over lowest heat until smooth and creamy.

Continue to cook until mixture begins to boil. Boil for 3 minutes and remove from heat.

Allow peanut butter mixture to cool to 100 degrees.

Add in chopped Xocai® Nuggets and stir until chocolate is melted throughout, and fudge is creamy and shiny.

Continue stirring until fudge begins to "set." The shine will begin to fade, and the fudge will thicken noticeably.

Transfer to a lightly "buttered" 8" square pan, spreading evenly.

Refrigerate overnight, or until fudge is set. Cut into 36 squares and serve.

See photos and tutorial of this recipe online at:

http://www.sexyveganmama.com/2012/05/xocai-vegan-peanut-butter-fudge.html

CINNAMON ROLLS AND DESSERT BREADS

Sexy Vegan Mama's Pumpkin Cinnamon Rolls

Christina-Marie's family loves cinnamon rolls, but she thinks they're sort of...*yawn*.

One day when shopping for ingredients for pumpkin pie, she picked up 30 ounces of pumpkin-pie filling instead of merely the 15 ounces called for by the pie recipe, reasoning, "I'm nothing, if not cheap, and can surely find some use for the extra 15 ounces".

What she ended up doing was a miraculous revamping of tired old cinnamon rolls.

1⅛ c. warm water ("baby bath water" warm—not too hot, or you'll kill the yeast)
1½ T. dry yeast
2 T. oil
1 - 15 oz. can pumpkin pie filling
6 to 7 c. unbleached flour
1 T. salt
2 T. cane sugar crystals or natural sugar
2 to 4 T. vegan stick margarine, softened

¼ c. cane sugar crystals or natural sugar
1 t. ground cinnamon

Glaze:

Blend until smooth or desired consistency:
2 to 3 c. organic powdered sugar
2 to 3 T. vanilla soy milk
Add more organic powdered sugar or soy milk if necessary.

Preheat oven to 375 degrees.

In a medium bowl, sprinkle yeast over water and allow to dissolve.

Add oil and pumpkin, mixing thoroughly.

In a large bowl, combine and mix flour, salt and 2 tablespoons cane juice crystals or sugar.

Make a "well" in the middle of the dry mixture, and then add liquid mixture.

Stir liquid into flour until it's too stiff to stir with a spoon, then oil hands and knead the dough.

Add more flour or water if necessary to achieve desired consistency. Dough should be slightly sticky, but not completely clinging to hands or bowl.

When dough forms easily into a ball, remove from

bowl, put about 1 teaspoon of oil into the bottom of the bowl, and roll the ball of dough in the oil to coat it.

Cover with a damp towel and allow to rise until doubled in size—about 1 hour.

Punch the dough down, divide in ½ and roll out on a floured board into two large rectangles—about 15" x 9".

Spread a layer of softened margarine over each rectangle.

Mix remaining cane juice crystals or sugar and cinnamon, and then sprinkle over "buttered" rectangles.

Starting at the wide end, roll the dough tightly into a long roll.

Slice, using a serrated knife, into 12 rolls. Place rolls into oiled muffin tins and let rise for about 20 minutes.

Bake 20 to 30 minutes, until golden brown on top.

Top with Glaze while warm.

See photos and tutorial for this recipe online at:

http://www.sexyveganmama.com/2010/11/sexy-vegan-mama-pumpkin-cinnamon-rolls.html

Whole Wheat Cinnamon Rolls That Don't Suck

Don't worry, we're not going all-out health nuts on you. We've simply created a cinnamon roll for the masses who love a good, hearty whole wheat bread. Substituting whole wheat for white flour is, at times, problematic in that it tends to produce drier, tougher finished products.

For this recipe, we alleviate the dryness by adding grated apple to the recipe, thereby making the dough less "thirsty," and providing a moist, dense finished roll. The recipe also relies on a bit more oil to keep it moist.

1¼ c. warm water ("baby bath water" warm—not too hot, or you'll kill the yeast)
1½ T. dry yeast
¼ c. oil
1 heaping cup grated apples (about 2 medium), packed
6 c. whole wheat flour
1 T. salt
¼ c. cane juice crystals or natural sugar
1 T. oil
2 to 4 T. vegan stick margarine, softened
¼ c. cane juice crystals or natural sugar
1 t. ground cinnamon

Glaze:

2 to 3 c. organic powdered sugar
2 to 3 T. vanilla soy milk

Add more powdered sugar or soy milk if necessary. Blend to desired smooth consistency.

Preheat oven to 375 degrees.

In a small bowl, sprinkle yeast over water and allow to dissolve.

Add oil and grated apples, mixing thoroughly.

In a large bowl, combine and mix flour, salt, and ¼ cup cane juice crystals or sugar.

Make a "well" in the middle of the dry mixture, and then add liquid mixture.

Stir liquid into flour until it's too stiff to stir with a spoon, then oil hands and knead the dough.

Add more flour or water if necessary to achieve desired consistency. Dough should be slightly sticky, but not completely clinging to hands or bowl. When dough forms easily into a ball, remove from bowl, put a Tablespoon of oil into the bottom of the bowl, and roll the ball of dough in the oil to coat it.

Cover with a damp towel and allow to rise until doubled in size—about 1 hour.

Punch the dough down, divide in half and roll out on a floured board into 2 large rectangles—about 15" x 9".

Spread a layer of softened margarine over each rectangle.

Mix remaining cane juice crystals or sugar, and cinnamon, and then sprinkle over "buttered" rectangles.

Starting at the wide end, roll the dough tightly into a long roll.

Slice each roll, using a serrated knife, into 12 sections. Place the sections, cut sides creating the tops and bottoms, into oiled muffin tins and let rise for about 20 minutes.

Bake until edges begin to brown, about 20 to 30 minutes.

Top with glaze while warm.

See photos and tutorial of this recipe online at:

http://www.sexyveganmama.com/2011/07/recipe-whole wheat-cinnamon-rolls-that.html

Bodacious Banana Bread

4 bananas (mashed)
1½ c. cane juice crystals or natural sugar
1 T. egg replacer, beaten with 4 T. water
½ c. oil
2 t. vanilla extract

2 c. oats
4 c. all-purpose baking mix
1 c. chopped nuts (optional)

Preheat oven to 350 degrees

Mix ingredients together in the order listed.

Pour batter into 2 large well-greased loaf pans

Bake for 55 to 60 minutes

Variations on baking times for different-sized pans:

3 medium loaf pans – Bake at 375 degrees for 30 minutes
4 small loaf pans – Bake at 375 degrees for 25 minutes
1 tube/bundt cake pan—Bake at 375 degrees for 55 minutes
24 regular muffin cups – Bake at 400 degrees for 20 minutes
12 large muffin cups – Bake at 400 degrees for 25 minutes

Blueberry Orange Bread

5 c. all-purpose baking mix
1 t. nutmeg
½ t. cinnamon
2 c. cane juice crystals or natural sugar
½ t. baking soda

1 T. orange peel (optional)
1 c. orange juice
1 T. egg replacer, beaten with 4 T. water
1 c. oil
2 c. blueberries

Preheat oven to 350 degrees

Mix ingredients together in the order listed. Do not over-mix blueberries.

Pour batter into two large well-greased loaf pans

Bake for 55 to 60 minutes

Variations on baking times for different-sized pans:

3 medium loaf pans – Bake at 375 degrees for 30 minutes
4 small loaf pans – Bake at 375 degrees for 25 minutes
1 tube/bundt cake pan – Bake at 375 degrees for 55 minutes
24 regular muffin cups – Bake at 400 degrees for 20 minutes
12 large muffin cups – Bake at 400 degrees for 25 minutes

"Zavory" Zucchini Bread

1½ c. shredded zucchini (1 medium)
¾ c. cane juice crystals or natural sugar

½ c. oil
1½ T. egg replacer powder, beaten with 6 T. water
3 t. cinnamon
2 t. nutmeg
2 c. all-purpose baking mix
½ c. chopped nuts (optional)

Preheat oven to 350 degrees.

Grease the bottom of a 9" x 5" x 3" loaf pan.

Mix together all ingredients except the baking mix and nuts. Blend well.

Add baking mix and beat with electric mixer on medium speed for 1 minute or until well blended.

Fold in nuts, if desired.

Bake 50 to 55 minutes or until toothpick inserted in center comes out clean.

Cool 10 minutes.

Loosen bread from sides of pan and remove. Place on wire rack until completely cooled before slicing (about 2 hours).

VEGAN BLOGS THE COOL KIDS READ

Andrea's Easy Vegan Cooking—http://cookeasyvegan.blogspot.com/
Bankrupt Vegan—http://bankruptvegan.blogspot.com/
Blessed Vegan Life—http://blessedveganlife.blogspot.com/
Bread Without Butter—http://breadwithoutbutter.blogspot.com/
C'est La Vegan—http://www.cestlavegan.com/
Cadry's Kitchen—http://cadryskitchen.com/
Carrie on Vegan—http://www.carrieonvegan.com/
Chic Vegan—http://chicvegan.com/
Cookin' Vegan—http://www.cookinvegan.com/
Cooking the Vegan Books—http://cookingtheveganbooks.com/
Crazy Sexy Life—http://crazysexylife.com/
Cupcake Kitteh—http://cupcakekitteh.blogspot.com/
Cupcakes and Kale—http://cupcakesandkale.blogspot.com/
Epicurean Vegan—http://epicureanvegan.com/
Fat Gay Vegan—http://fatgayvegan.com/

FatFree Vegan Kitchen—http://blog.fatfreevegan.com/

Feed Me I'm Cranky—http://www.feedmeimcranky.com/

Finding Vegan—http://www.findingvegan.com/

Fragrant Vanilla Cake—http://fragrantvanillacake.blogspot.com/

Fresh Young Coconut—http://freshyoungcoconut.blogspot.com/

Happy Herbivore—http://happyherbivore.com/blog/

Happy, Healthy, Life—http://kblog.lunchboxbunch.com/

Holy Cow! Vegan Recipes—http://www.holy-cowvegan.net/

Hungry Vegan—http://hungryvegan.blogspot.com/

In-A-Gadda-Da-Vegan—http://blogs.standard.net/in-a-gadda-da-vegan/

JL Goes Vegan—http://jlgoesvegan.com/

Kirsten's Kitchen of Vegan Creations—http://kirstenskitchen.blogspot.com/

Manifest Vegan—http://www.manifestvegan.com/

Mighty Vegan—http://www.mightyvegan.com/

New Orleans in Green—http://neworleansingreen.blogspot.com/

Nom! Nom! Nom!—http://nomnomnomblog.com/

Olives for Dinner—http://www.olivesfordinner.blogspot.com/

Opera Singer in the Kitchen—http://www.singer-skitchen.com/

Oy Vegan—http://oyvegan.com/

Plant-Powered Kitchen—http://plantpoweredkitchen.com/blog/
Post Punk Kitchen—http://www.theppk.com/
Pride and Vegudice—http://prideandvegudice.com/
Quarrygirl—http://www.quarrygirl.com/
RAWk Me!—http://rawgirlinmumbai.blogspot.com/
Sarah's Place—http://www.govegan.net/
Scissors and Spice—http://www.scissorsandspice.com/
Sexy Vegan Mama (that's my blog, yo!)—http://sexyveganmama.com
Spa Bettie—http://spabettie.com/
Spice Island Vegan—http://spiceislandvegan.blogspot.com/
That Normal Vegan—http://www.thatnormalvegan.com/
That Pain in the Ass Vegan—http://thatpaonintheass-vegan.blogspot.com/
That Was Vegan?—http://thatwasvegan.wordpress.com/
The Chubby Vegan—http://www.thechubbyvegan.com/
The Streets I Know: A Vegan Fashion Blog—http://streetsiknow.blogspot.com/
The Sweetest Vegan—http://thesweetestvegan.com/
The Tasty Vegan—http://www.thetastyvegan.com/
The Tolerant Vegan—http://thetolerantvegan.com/
The Tropical Vegan—http://travelingvegan.blogspot.com/
The Vegan Butcher—http://www.theveganbutcher.

com/
The Vegan Stoner—http://theveganstoner.blogspot.com/
The Vegan Version—http://www.theveganversion.com/
Urban Vegan—http://urbanvegan.net/
Veg TV—http://www.vegtv.com/
Vegan Chai—http://veganchai.wordpress.com/
Vegan Chicks Rock—http://veganchicksrock.blogspot.com/
Vegan Crunk—http://vegancrunk.blogspot.com/
Vegan Culinary Crusade—http://www.veganculinary-crusade.com/
Vegan Dad—http://vegandad.blogspot.com/
Vegan Eats—http://veganeatsblog.com/
Vegan Eats & Treats—http://veganeatsandtreats.blogspot.com/
Vegan Food for the Hungry Student—http://vegan-foodforhungrystudents.blogspot.com/
Vegan Good Things—http://www.vegangoodthings.blogspot.com/
Vegan Lunch Box—http://veganlunchbox.blogspot.com/
Vegan Mommy Chef—http://veganmommychef.blogspot.com/
Vegan Planet—http://veganplanet.blogspot.com/
Vegan Thyme—http://veganthyme.blogspot.com/
Vegan Vagrant—http://veganvagrant.com/
Vegan Vice—http://www.veganvice.blogspot.com/
Vegan Victuals—http://www.veganvictuals.com/

blog/
Vegan YumYum—http://veganyumyum.com
Vegangela—http://www.vegangela.com/
Veganlicious LJ—http://veganliciouslj.tumblr.com/
Vegansaurus—http://vegansaurus.com/
Vegenista—http://vegenista.com/
Veggie Converter—http://veggieconverter.com/
Veggie Wedgie—http://www.veggie-wedgie.com/
Veggieful—http://www.veggieful.com/
Vegtastic Voyage—http://vegtasticvoyage.com/
Yeah, That "Vegan" Shit—http://yeahthatveganshit.blogspot.com/
Your Vegan Mom—http://www.yourveganmom.com/

GET SCHOOLED: ONLINE VEGAN RESOURCES

All Recipes Vegan – recipes, online community, tips and nutrition information—http://allrecipesvegan.com/

Barnivore.com – guide to vegan beer, wine and liquor—http://www.barnivore.com/

Forks Over Knives – nutrition and diet information pertaining to how a vegan diet may stop or even reverse degenerative diseases—http://www.forksoverknives.com/

Is It Vegan? – answers to questions about whether or not particular foods are vegan—http://www.isitvegan.com/

Mercy for Animals – vegetarian/vegan starter kit—http://www.mercyforanimals.org/

Northwest Veg – events, newsletters, restaurant listings, nutrition information, Veg 101, garden resources, publication recommendations and more—http://nwveg.org/

The Vegan Society – lifestyle and nutrition, news and events, shopping recommendations and more—http://www.vegansociety.com/

TryVeg.com – vegetarian starter guide, recipes, product recommendations, news and education—http://www.tryveg.com/

Vegan Outreach – vegan starter guide, FAQs on veganism, recipes and education—http://www.veganoutreach.org/

Vegan Voice – events, food, humor—http://thevegan-voice.org/

Vegan World Order – user-submitted recipes, restaurant listings, and more—http://www.veganworldorder.com/

Vegan.com – info, shopping, recipes and more—http://www.vegan.com/

VeganMoFo – Vegan Month of Food—http://VeganMoFo.wordpress.com

Vegetarian Resource Group – nutrition information, recipes, resources for teens and families, guides and handouts, restaurant listings and much more—http://www.vrg.org/

VegNews – articles, recipes, product reviews, vegan guides, tips, shopping, vegan starter kits and news-letters—http://vegnews.com/

VegVine – Vegan Health 101, veg starter kit, recipes and health information—http://www.vegvine.com/

Vegweb – user-submitted recipes—http://vegweb.com

Viva! – "Vegan Basics" guide—http://www.vivausa.org/veganbasics/

Worldwide Vegan Bake Sale – information about the

annual Worldwide Vegan Bake Sale, links to vegan dessert and baking blogs, introduction to veganism, vegan literature and bake sale tips—http://www.veganbakesale.org/

ACKNOWLEDGEMENTS AND SHOUT-OUTS

Christina-Marie would like to thank:

Mr. Wright, Princess, The Dude, Pockets, Pepper, GirlWonder, Curlytop and Snugglebug for being taste-testers, letting her lock herself in her room to write sometimes, and for doing the dishes.

My co-author, William Maltese, for nearly-limitless patience and providing Xocai® Nuggets for recipe development.

My parents (who are not yet sainted, but ought to be shoo-ins after raising me), and Granny, who spent a lifetime in the kitchen, and was kind enough to pass down recipes and the "baking gene" to her granddaughter.

Nick and Teresa at Bear Foods in Chelan, Washington (http://www.bearfoodsmarket.com/) for ordering in every little thing my vegan heart desires when the baking bug bites, and for fueling my body many afternoons at the creperie.

Tara Kalian at Lulu Boutique (http://luluchelan.com) for providing Xocai® Chocolate for recipe development. Sorry your staff ate all the samples before you could taste them, Tara!

Tiffany at Bread Without Butter (http://breadwithoutbutter.blogspot.com/) for recipe testing, feedback, and blogging like a BOSS!

Catherine Burt at In-A-Gadda-Da-Vegan (http://blogs.standard.net/in-a-gadda-da-vegan/) for story sharing, recipe testing and feedback—and for being an amazing advocate for animals and vegans.

Jenn at Cookin' Vegan (http://www.cookinvegan.com/) for recipe testing, feedback, and sending me delightful vegan treats in the mail.

Kris Miller (http://dustpanproductions.com) for her contributions, recipe feedback, and for being a generally all-around awesome person.

Kristie Arnold (http://VeggieConverter.com) for her contributions, being a faithful Twitter pal, drooling over my recipes and blog posts, and pretty much being very cool in every way.

Natalie at Vegitate (http://vegitate.blogspot.com) for emailing me her feedback on recipes.

Kyle Domer (http://VeganVagrant.com) for being so swagalicious, and telling his personal story.

Robbie Gleeson (http://twitter.com/itsjustrobbieok) for sharing his story of raw veganism.

Tracye Mayolo for detailing her personal journey to veganism and being an absolute sweetheart.

Readers at SexyVeganMama.com for commenting, drooling, and—oh, yes—reading.

Anyone and everyone else I forgot to thank—and

I'm sure there are many. I'd totally suck at one of those Academy Award speeches.

William would like to thank:

Pamela Hoffman, my sister and friend, who seems always ready and able to provide me with an extra pair of eyes for preparing a manuscript for publication.

Bonnie Clark, Adrienne Z. Milligan, Cecile Charles, and A.B. Gayle, all fellow authors with me in cook-, diet-, and wine-book collaborations, who have made me more aware of foods, a better cook, and a far superior wine connoisseur than I would have been without them.

Robert Reginald, John Betancourt, and the rest of the staff at Wildside Press/Borgo Press who make "The Traveling Gourmand" series possible.

ABOUT THE AUTHORS: YOU CAN'T MAKE THIS STUFF UP

Christina-Marie (Sexy Vegan Mama) Wright is the manic mother of seven, wife to a real estate professional and political activist (the same guy—Mr. Wright) and author of the hilarious *EVERYTHING I NEED TO KNOW ABOUT MOTHERHOOD I LEARNED FROM ANIMAL HOUSE*, available on Amazon.

After giving birth to one child—just to see if her body worked—she picked up four full-time stepchildren and two adopted children along her zigzagging path to (near) self-actualization. Her family isn't "blended." It's "pureed."

That frothy blend of maternal mayhem includes: Princess (stepdaughter, b. 1990, Veterinary Medicine student), The Dude (stepson, b. 1993, employed, living on his own), Pockets (bio son, b. 1994, attending college), Pepper (stepdaughter, b. 1996, high school diva), GirlWonder (stepdaughter, b. 1997, middle school over-achiever), Curlytop (adopted daughter, b. 2005, special needs child allergic to Red Dye 40, diagnosed Sensory Processing Disorder) and Snugglebug (adopted daughter, b. 2006, diagnosed Sensory Processing Disorder, also allergic to Red Dye 40).

A vegan for over 15 years, and a Washington state native, Christina-Marie makes her home along the Columbia River, and the view from her living room is better than yours.

She's also a sexual health consultant, and absolutely capable of teaching you how to find your G-spot.

You can find Christina-Marie hanging out with a snifter of Southern Comfort at Christina-MarieWright.com, TheGonzoMama.com and SexyVeganMama.com.

William Maltese is the best-selling author of not only his cookbook series that presently includes his *THE GLUTEN FREE-WAY, MY WAY* (with Adrienne Z. Hoffman), *BACK OF THE BOAT COOKING* and *EVEN GOURMANDS HAVE TO DIET* (both with Bonnie Clark), and *DINNER WITH WILLIAM AND CECILE: COOKBOOK* (with Cecile Charles), but, also, his *WILLIAM MALTESE'S WINE TASTER'S DIARY SERIES* that presently includes *SPOKANE/PULLMAN WA WINE REGION* and *IN SEARCH OF THE PERFECT G IN AUSTRALIA'S MORNINGINGTON PENINSULA* (the latter with A.B. Gayle), all for "The Traveling Gourmand" imprint of Wildside/Borgo Press.

William, who can be heard weekly on his radio show *NO BOUNDARIES*, received a B.A. in Marketing/Advertising, and served an honorable term of service in the U.S. Army where he achieved the rank of E-5.

He started his writing career in men's pulp magazines, and has since published more than 200 books, fiction and non-fiction, in every genre, having been honored with a listing in the prestigious *WHO'S WHO IN AMERICA*.

For a more comprehensive overview of William and his impressive body of work, see the reference volume *DRAQUALIAN SILK: A COLLECTOR'S AND BIBLIOGRAPHICAL GUIDE TO THE BOOKS OF WILLIAM MALTESE, 1969-2012*, available through bookstores everywhere.

Contact William via email at:
maltese@yahoo.com

Tune in to his cohosting of the *NO BOUNDARIES* podcast, every Wednesday, 7:00 P.M. Eastern at:
http://www.noboundariesradioshow.com

Or find him on the internet at:
http://www.williammaltese.com
http://www.facebook.com/williammaltese
http://www.mxi.myvoffice.com/williammaltese
(for Xocai® chocolate)
http://friendzstop.com/magazine/contributors/william-maltese
http://www.theglutenfreewaymyway.com
http://www.myspace.com/williammaltese

www.ingramcontent.com/pod-product-compliance
Lightning Source LLC
LaVergne TN
LVHW041620070426
835507LV00008B/355